CONTENTS

Biba's
Northern Italian
Cooking

Biba Caggiano

HPBooks

HPBooks
Published by The Berkley Publishing Group
A division of Penguin Putnam Inc.
375 Hudson Street
New York, New York 10014

Copyright © 2002 by Biba Caggiano
Text design by Tiffany Kukec
Cover design by Dawn Velez Le Bron
Cover photo of author by Robert Olding Photography/View Magazine

First edition: January 2002
Published simultaneously in Canada.

Visit our website at www.penguinputnam.com

Library of Congress Cataloging-in-Publication Data

Caggiano, Biba.
    Biba's Northern Italian cooking / Biba Caggiano.—1st ed.
        p. cm.
    Includes index.
    ISBN 1-55788-380-7
    I. Title.

    TX723.2.N65 C32 2002
    641.5945—dc21
                                                    2001051658

Printed in the United States of America

10   9   8   7   6   5   4   3   2

Fabulous Food of Northern Italy

I often ask myself: How did I become a cook? And most of all, where does this passion and devotion to good food come from? I suppose, it all began in Bologna, the city of my birth and my youth, a city well known all over Italy for the unsurpassed excellence of its food.

I was literally raised in the kitchen because the kitchen was, at that time, the center and soul of the house. My mother was a great cook. Her food was the simple, straightforward dishes of the area, loaded with aroma and taste, and she prepared it daily with an abundance of love. So, I can truthfully say, that I was raised on a great diet. Good food and love.

When I moved to New York to follow my American-born husband, this heritage of food stayed with me. For almost eight years I worked outside the home, took care of the house and prepared meals for my husband. Then we moved to Sacramento, California, where my time was spent raising our daughters, Carla and Paola, taking care of the house and doing a great deal of cooking for family and friends.

Upon the insistence of some friends, I held my first cooking class in my kitchen in 1977. Within a few years I was teaching very popular classes in Sacramento and all over California. The food of Northern Italy, with its enormous range, simplicity and great classic dishes, had won the hearts of my students. They went home and cooked. They made gnocchi, polenta, pasta and risotto. They learned at the classes and in their own kitchen that northern Italian food is simply outstanding and outstandingly simple.

Anyone who has traveled to Italy will tell you that Italian cuisine is unbelievably varied. Before the unification of Italy in 1861, each city-state had different rulers, cultures, customs and dialects. Each also had its distinctive cuisine. Italian food has its roots drawn from peasant cooking. However, for centuries Italy has had popes, courts and great families who have brought a more sophisticated and lavish style to the cuisine. The blending of these two styles of cooking has resulted in *la buona cucina casalinga*, good home cooking.

The cooking styles of northern Italy are as diversified as the Italian landscape. The cooking of Piedmont, for example, is very different from the cooking of Emilia-Romagna. Piedmont is dominated by mountains. Its cuisine is robust, sober and elegant. Game, truffles and meats braised in full-bodied wines are all part of Piedmont cooking. This region is also the greatest producer of rice in Europe.

By contrast, Emilia-Romagna is located in one of the flattest parts of Italy with the Appenines in the northwest and the Adriatic Sea to the east. This area is known for its generous use of butter and for pork products that find their way into innumerable dishes. Emilia-Romagna leads Italy in the production of wheat and consequently is famous for the quality of its homemade pasta.

Cooking is second nature for most Italians. Even though certain guidelines are important, there is no place in Italian cooking for rigid rules or formulas. The love of cooking and eating is reflected in everyday life. Shopping is generally done daily to assure the freshest possible ingredients. Great care is taken in the selection of these ingredients. The Italian cook takes her daily meals seriously. By 11 A.M. she is preparing a sauce or a ragù to be served over pasta at 1 P.M. The country shuts down daily at 12:30 P.M. every day. Italians jump into their cars and fight the chaotic city traffic to reach their homes in order to enjoy lunch, the most important meal of the day, with their families.

Serving a meal properly is almost as important as cooking it well. In an Italian meal, portions are generally small. Pasta, soup, risotto or gnocchi is served as a first course. A small portion of meat or fish with some vegetables follows. Then a simple salad is served dressed with a bit of olive oil and vinegar. Fresh fruit and espresso might end the meal. Desserts are only served on special occasions.

The evening meal is generally much lighter. Often it consists of a clear broth soup, followed by a bit of fish or meat or by a salad and perhaps some cheese.

Today, more than ever, Italian cooking is at everyone's fingertips because of the availability of Italian ingredients. Extra-virgin olive oils, cheeses, wild mushrooms, rice, sun-dried tomatoes, balsamic vinegar, prosciutto and great factory-made pasta, can be found almost anywhere. Keep in mind that Italian cuisine is a skillful blending of ingredients that complement each other. Once you have done that, you will have mastered the art of Italian cooking.

Some Basic Ingredients

Because Italian cuisine is basically simple, each ingredient plays a very important role. Certain dishes cannot be made without a specific ingredient and still be considered authentic. While many ingredients are vital, I also realize that some are often unavailable in smaller towns. I urge you to go the extra mile to find an important ingredient and to substitute only if you must.

BASIL: Fresh basil is probably the most popular Italian herb. The only substitute is home-preserved basil. Basil leaves can be preserved between layers of coarse salt in tightly sealed jars. They lose some of their green color, but retain the favor. Basil can also be preserved in olive oil.

BROTH: Broth is an important ingredient in Italian cooking. Risotto, for example, cannot be made without it. Broth is also used in sauces, stews and braised meats. Make large batches and freeze it.

BUTTER: Butter is widely used in Northern Italy. It is preferred for cooking instead of olive. I prefer to use unsalted butter.

FONTINA CHEESE: Fontina is a delicious cheese from Piedmont. Its delicate flavor enhances many Italian dishes. Substitute with stronger-flavored Danish fontina only if absolutely necessary.

GARLIC: Garlic is widely used in Italian cooking, but it should not be abused. Many dishes that call for garlic need only a hint of it. Choose a large head of garlic with firm, unwrinkled cloves.

GORGONZOLA CHEESE: This blue-vein cheese comes from Lombardy. Gorgonzola is pungent with a creamy consistency. Substitute blue cheese, preferably Oregon Blue, only if absolutely necessary.

MARSALA WINE: The best Marsala wine comes from Marsala in Sicily. Dry and sweet types are available. Use dry Marsala for cooking. Its aromatic flavor is essential to many dishes. American Marsala wine is sweeter than the Italian and should be used with discretion. Substitute dry sherry if Marsala is unavailable.

MOZZARELLA CHEESE: One of Italy's favorite cheeses, the best mozzarella is made from the curd of water-buffalo milk. It is generally stored in water and does not keep very long. It has a creamy and delicate taste. Substitute domestic mozzarella.

OIL FOR FRYING: For deep-frying use any light-flavored vegetable oil.

OLIVE OIL: In choosing an olive oil, look for a nice green color and a pleasing taste and fragrance. Some of the best Italian olive oils come from Tuscany, Umbria and Liguria. Extra-virgin olive oil, which is the product of the first pressing of the olives, is considered the best. Store olive oil in a tightly capped bottle in a cool, dark place. Use olive oil within a few months or it may turn rancid.

PANCETTA: Pancetta is the same cut of pork as bacon. It is cured with salt and is not smoked. It comes rolled up like a large salami. Widely used in Italian cooking, especially in Emilia-Romagna, it is vital to many dishes. If available, buy a large quantity, cut into several pieces and freeze it. You can substitute domestic bacon for pancetta, but it must be blanched in boiling water for two to three minutes to reduce the smoky flavor. Fresh side pork can also be used.

PARMESAN CHEESE: Italian cuisine would not be the same without this cheese. Parmesan is produced in an area between Parma and Reggio-Emilia. It is made under strict regulations. When buying Parmesan, look for *Parmigiano Reggiano* stamped on the crust. The cheese should be straw-yellow and crumbly and moist inside. It is expensive, but a little goes a long way. Buy a small piece and grate only what you need. Wrap the remaining cheese tightly in foil and store in the refrigerator. Domestic Parmesan is subject to different standards and not aged as long. If necessary, domestic Parmesan can be used. Do not use the grated Parmesan sold at the supermarket unless you have no other choice.

PARSLEY: If available, use the large, flat-leaf Italian parsley. Parsley is widely used in Italian cooking. It is a good source of vitamins A and C and also iron.

PROSCIUTTO: Prosciutto is uncooked, unsmoked ham. It is salted, air-cured and aged a minimum of one year. Italian prosciutto is usually much sweeter than the American counterpart. Prosciutto is widely used in Italian cooking and as an antipasto. Domestic prosciutto is an acceptable substitute.

RICE: Italian rice is short and thick-grained. It is perfect for risotto. Imported Italian rice such as *arborio* is available in Italian groceries and specialty stores. California short-grain pearl rice can be substituted for arborio.

RICOTTA CHEESE: Domestic ricotta is acceptable. It has a creamier consistency than Italian ricotta and is more watery. Never substitute cottage cheese for ricotta.

ROSEMARY: Rosemary is deliciously aromatic. It is excellent with roasts or in marinades. Dried rosemary is perfectly acceptable.

SAGE: Sage is at its best when used with poultry and game. Use dried sage sparingly because its strong flavor can be overwhelming.

TOMATOES: There is no doubt that a sauce made from meaty sun-ripened tomatoes is unbeatable. Good-quality canned tomatoes make a good substitute. If possible, choose an imported Italian variety. If using domestic canned plum tomatoes, try several brands to find one that suits your taste.

VINEGAR: Use a good, unflavored wine vinegar.

WILD ITALIAN MUSHROOMS: These are one of the glorious elements in Italian gastronomy. They grow under chestnut trees and are abundant in the fall and spring. Drying wild mushrooms preserves their distinctive flavor. Dried wild Italian mushrooms are available in Italian groceries and gourmet stores.

WINE: If a wine is good enough to drink, it is good enough for cooking. Do not use cheap wine for cooking because the flavor of the dish can be altered by the quality of the wine.

Appetizers

*A*ntipasto means "before the pasta." In the daily family meals, antipasti do not play a very important role. When people entertain or dine out in restaurants, antipasti become the exciting prelude to a special meal. At home, a simple antipasto generally consists of a few slices of sweet prosciutto or local salami, served with ripe cantaloupe or figs. Prosciutto and melon are the ideal antipasto because they make a light and delicate combination.

An antipasto should never be overpowering in flavor or quantity. It should only tease the palate, leaving you with a desire for more. The same rule should be applied when considering an antipasto for entertaining. An antipasto should be planned to complement the meal that will follow. Bear in mind also the wines that will be served. Don't serve an antipasto containing vinegar if a wine is served with it. Vinegar destroys the taste of wine.

In Italy, the best place to see antipasti displayed is in a restaurant. Italians believe that first you eat with your eyes, then with your palate. This is especially true in an Italian restaurant where antipasti are arranged on a large table or appetizer cart. One look at those mouthwatering presentations and your willpower is washed away. Even in the indulgence of a special evening, don't forget the meal that will follow. Select an antipasto that will complement rather than overpower the meal.

Italian antipasti are extremely versatile. They often originate in the imagination of a good cook rather than the pages of a cookbook. Carefully selected antipasti can be served as summer buffets, late suppers or for an impromptu gathering of friends and family. An array of fresh vegetables dipped in olive oil and lemon can either start or end a meal. A cold meat dish such as

Cold Veal in Tuna Sauce, page 154, is equally acceptable as an antipasto or an elegant main course.

Most antipasti in this book can be prepared in very little time with a minimum of effort. Some can be prepared ahead. Feel free to improvise. Pay particular attention to the presentation and your meal will be off to a perfect start.

GRILLED PORCINI CAPS

Porcini alla Griglia

In spring and fall when wild mushrooms abound, fresh porcini in Italy are everywhere. These mushrooms with their nut-brown color and meaty caps, are most delicious when grilled, basted simply with extra-virgin olive oil and seasoned with salt and pepper. If you can't find porcini, look for large capped portobello or portabella, and grill them as you would porcini.

MAKES 4 SERVINGS

1½ pounds fresh porcini mushrooms, or portabella mushrooms
⅓ cup extra-virgin olive oil
Salt and freshly ground black pepper

2 tablespoons chopped fresh flat leaf Italian parsley, combined with
1 small garlic clove, finely minced

Preheat grill or an outdoor barbecue.

Remove stalks of mushrooms and dark gills and discard. Clean mushrooms thoroughly with a damp towel. Brush mushroom caps on both sides with olive oil and season generously with salt and pepper. Place caps on hot grill and cook, turning them a few times and brushing them with oil, until they are tender, approximately 7 to 8 minutes.

Place caps on individual serving dishes, sprinkle them with parsley and garlic and drizzle with a bit more oil. Serve hot.

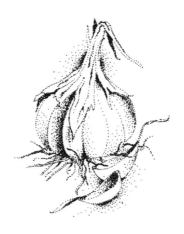

PIETRO'S MORTADELLA MOUSSE

La Spuma di Mortadella di Pietro

Pietro was for many years the chef of Diana, the most venerable restaurant of Bologna. Every time I had dinner there he would bring to the table a small plate of mortadella crostini. Now that mortadella has finally been imported in this country, I can prepare these crostini and serve them before dinner, with a nice glass of chilled white wine or aperitif.

MAKES 6 TO 8 SERVINGS

½ pound piece mortadella
⅓ cup freshly grated Parmigiano-
   Reggiano cheese
¼ pound ricotta cheese
Salt to taste

⅓ cup Chicken Broth, page 23, or low-
   sodium canned
½ cup heavy cream, whipped
12 to 14 slices firm-textured white bread

Cut mortadella into pieces and place in a food processor fitted with the metal blade. Process until mortadella is very finely chopped. Add Parmigiano and ricotta and season lightly with salt. With motor running pour in broth through feed tube until mortadella is completely pureed and mixture is thoroughly blended. Place mixture in a medium bowl and fold in cream.

Transfer mousse into a small, attractive serving bowl, cover with plastic wrap and refrigerate 2 to 3 hours or overnight. Leave mousse about 1 hour at room temperature before serving.

To serve, preheat oven to 400F (205C). Lightly oil a baking sheet. Trim crust from bread and cut each slice of bread with a 2-inch-round cookie cutter, or cut them into triangles or rectangles. Arrange bread on baking sheet and place on middle rack of oven. Bake until bread has a light golden color. Turn pieces and brown other side, about 5 minutes.

Place bowl with mousse on a large, round dish and serve with toasted bread for spreading.

Variation
For a firmer mousse, use 1 teaspoon gelatin dissolved in 4 tablespoons water, then melt gelatin in a double boiler until it is clear of any lumps and stir it into mortadella mixture.

Tip
Mortadella can be found in Italian delicatessens and specialty food stores. Substitute baked or boiled ham if unavailable.

SWORDFISH CARPACCIO WITH ARUGULA

Carpaccio di Pesce Spada

Da Pippo, a small trattoria in Cesenatico, is where I enjoyed this delicious swordfish carpaccio. Pale pink flesh of thinly sliced swordfish had been marinated with shallots, lemon juice and olive oil, and was topped by small leaves of bright, green arugula. Make sure to choose the freshest fish, freshest arugula, and a flavorful, light, golden extra-virgin olive oil.

MAKES 4 SERVINGS

4 (¼-inch-thick) large slices swordfish, about ¾ pound

Salt to taste

1 to 2 tablespoons very finely minced shallots

Juice of 1 large lemon

½ cup extra-virgin olive oil

½ pound arugula, thoroughly washed and stems removed

Place swordfish slices between 2 large sheets of plastic wrap, and pound them gently until they are thin, almost transparent. (Don't pound them too thin or they might break as you pick them up.) Put slices on individual serving dishes. Season with salt and sprinkle with minced shallots. Dribble some lemon juice and about half of oil over each slice, cover plates with plastic wrap and refrigerate 1 to 2 hours.

Put arugula in a bowl and season with salt. Toss salad with remaining oil and a few drops of lemon juice. Pile a small mound of arugula over swordfish and serve.

CALAMARI SALAD

Calamari in Insalata

Seafood salads are pretty much standard in restaurants and trattorie of Romagna's seacoast. Whether they are made with one or several types of fish, they all have one thing in common: simplicity. The freshest seafood possible, the most flavorful olive oil, only a whiff of garlic and a few drops of lemon juice are all it takes to make this salad outstanding.

MAKES 4 SERVINGS

1 recipe Vegetable Broth, page 24

3 pounds calamari (squid), smallest you can find, cleaned as directed on page 107, or 2 pounds cleaned squid

1 garlic clove, peeled and halved

1½ cups diced, tender white celery stalks

1 tablespoon chopped fresh flat-leaf Italian parsley

Salt to taste

¼ to ⅓ cup extra-virgin olive oil

3 to 4 tablespoons lemon juice

Prepare Vegetable Broth. Strain it and set aside until ready to use.

When you are ready to poach calamari, bring broth back to a full boil. Add calamari, turn heat off and let them sit in hot broth about 2 minutes. Drain calamari and place in a bowl of ice water to stop cooking. Drain again, pat dry with paper towels, then cut sacs into ½-inch rings, and tentacles in half lengthwise.

Rub garlic all around inside of a salad bowl and add calamari. Cover bowl with plastic wrap and chill in refrigerator for about 1 hour.

Remove calamari from refrigerator. Add celery and parsley, season with salt and toss with oil and lemon juice. Leave salad at room temperature for about 30 minutes, taste, adjust seasonings and serve.

GRILLED MARINATED VEGETABLES

Verdure alla Griglia Marinate

Almost any vegetable can be used for this dish, which can be served as an appetizer or a side dish.

MAKES 4 SERVINGS

2 large red or yellow sweet peppers

1 small, firm eggplant

4 small zucchini

¼ cup red wine vinegar

½ cup olive oil plus extra for brushing

2 garlic cloves, finely minced

Salt and freshly ground pepper to taste

8 to 10 fresh basil leaves, finely shredded, or 1 tablespoon finely chopped fresh parsley

Roast and peel the peppers as instructed on page 18. Cut peeled peppers into large strips and place them slightly overlapping in a large, shallow serving dish. Cut off the ends of the eggplant and cut eggplant lengthwise into ½-inch-thick slices. Place slices in one layer on a large tray or dish, sprinkle with salt and let stand about 30 minutes. (The salt will draw out the eggplant's bitter juices.) Pat dry with paper towels. Cut ends off zucchini and slice in half lengthwise.

Preheat the broiler or the grill. Brush the eggplant and zucchini lightly with oil and place them under the broiler or on the grill until they are golden on both sides. Place them in the dish alongside the peppers. In a small bowl combine the vinegar, garlic, the ½ cup oil, salt, pepper and basil and mix well to combine. Taste and adjust the seasoning. Pour the dressing over the vegetables, leave at room temperature 30 to 40 minutes and serve.

BAKED ASPARAGUS WITH HAM

Involtini di Asparagi con Prosciutto Cotto

Demonstrate the versatility of Italian food by serving this as an appetizer, lunch or supper.

§ৡ **MAKES 4 SERVINGS**

1½ **pounds asparagus**
8 **slices boiled ham**

¼ **cup freshly grated Parmesan cheese**
2 **tablespoons butter**

Preheat oven to 350F (175C). Butter an 11 × 7-inch baking dish. Cut off tough asparagus ends. Using a sharp knife or potato peeler, peel outer skin from asparagus. Tie asparagus together in 1 or 2 bunches with string or rubber bands. Pour cold salted water 2 to 3 inches deep in an asparagus cooker, tall stockpot or old coffeepot. Place asparagus upright in water. Bring water to a boil. Cover and cook over high heat 6 to 8 minutes, depending on size. Drain on paper towels; remove string or rubber bands.

Divide asparagus into 4 bundles. Wrap 2 slices ham around each bundle. Arrange wrapped asparagus bundles in buttered baking dish in a single layer. Sprinkle with Parmesan cheese and dot with butter. Bake 8 to 10 minutes, or until cheese is melted.

MOZZARELLA AND TOMATOES WITH BASIL AND OIL

Mozzarella e Pomodori al Basilico e Olio

Italian mozzarella cheese, sun-ripened tomatoes and fresh basil; this is Italian food at its best.

§ৡ **MAKES 4 TO 6 SERVINGS**

4 **large firm tomatoes**
½ **pound mozzarella cheese, sliced**
10 **to 12 fresh basil leaves**

Salt and freshly ground pepper to taste
¼ **cup olive oil**

Wash and dry tomatoes. Cut into slices. On a large platter, alternate mozzarella cheese and tomato slices, slightly overlapping. Place a few basil leaves between slices. Refrigerate about 15 minutes. Season with salt and pepper. Drizzle with olive oil.

CROSTINI WITH ROASTED PEPPERS, CAPERS AND BASIL

Crostini con Peperoni Arrostiti, Capperi e Basilico

A simple, rustic, delicious appetizer, great for informal meals outdoors.

◯ MAKES 12 CROSTINI

4 large red or yellow sweet peppers

2 tablespoons capers, rinsed and patted
  dry

10 to 12 fresh basil leaves, finely
  shredded, or 1 tablespoon chopped
  fresh parsley

¼ cup extra-virgin olive oil

2 garlic cloves, finely minced

4 to 6 anchovy fillets, chopped

Salt to taste

12 (½-inch-thick) large slices crusty
  Italian bread

Roast and peel the peppers as instructed on page 18. Cut the peeled peppers into thin strips and place in a medium bowl. Add capers and basil. In a small bowl, combine oil, garlic and anchovies and mix well. Pour this dressing over the peppers and season lightly with salt. (Remember that anchovies are already quite salty.)

Preheat broiler. Put the bread on a broiler pan and place under the broiler. Broil until the slices are golden on both sides. (This step can be prepared several hours ahead of time.) Top each slice of bread with some of the pepper mixture, place on a serving platter and serve.

FRIED POLENTA WITH GORGONZOLA CHEESE

Crostini di Polenta Fritta

Prepare this dish a few hours ahead and put briefly under the broiler before serving.

◯ MAKES 6 TO 8 SERVINGS

Basic Polenta, page 86

6 ounces Gorgonzola cheese, at room
  temperature

3 tablespoons butter, at room
  temperature

1 tablespoon whipping cream

Oil for frying

Prepare Basic Polenta and let cool completely.

In a small bowl, mix Gorgonzola cheese, butter and cream until blended. Set aside.

Cut cooled polenta into slices 2 inches wide and 6 inches long. Pour oil about 1 inch deep in a large skillet. Heat oil until a 1-inch cube of bread turns golden almost immediately. Fry polenta slices over medium heat until golden, about 1 minute on each side. Drain on paper towels.

Spread cheese mixture over hot polenta slices. Place on a warm platter. Serve immediately.

ᘯ

BRUSCHETTA WITH FRESH TOMATOES AND BASIL

Bruschetta al Pomodoro

This rustic appetizer should be prepared only in summer, when ripe, juicy tomatoes are at their best.

MAKES 8 SERVINGS

8 (1-inch-thick) slices Italian bread
3 garlic cloves, sliced in half
½ cup extra-virgin olive oil

2 to 3 large ripe tomatoes, sliced
Salt and freshly ground pepper to taste
⅓ cup coarsely shredded fresh basil

Preheat oven to 400F (205C). Place the bread slices on a baking sheet and bake 8 to 10 minutes, or until they are golden on both sides.

Rub one side of the toasted bread with garlic and drizzle with a little oil. Arrange a few slices of tomatoes over each slice of bread, season with salt and pepper and sprinkle with some basil. Drizzle tomatoes with more of the oil and serve while still warm.

MIXED SEAFOOD SALAD

Insalata Mista di Mare

A great seafood salad needs only three things: fresh fish, a light hand in cooking it and flavorful extra-virgin olive oil.

❧ **MAKES 4 SERVINGS**

6 ounces bay scallops, rinsed under cold water

6 ounces medium shrimp, shelled and deveined

12 ounces white fish, such as halibut, mahi mahi or orange roughy, cut into 1½-inch pieces

3 ripe Roma tomatoes, diced

4 small green onions, white part only, thinly sliced

10 to 12 fresh basil leaves, shredded

Salt and freshly ground pepper to taste

2 garlic cloves, minced

⅓ cup extra-virgin olive oil

Juice of 1 large lemon

Crusty Italian bread

Bring a medium saucepan of water to a boil over medium heat; add scallops and shrimp. Cook 1½ to 2 minutes or until scallops are opaque and shrimp are pink. Remove with a slotted spoon and place in a bowl of very cold water to stop the cooking.

Add the fish pieces to the boiling water and cook 2 to 2½ minutes, or until the fish is opaque all the way through. Remove with a slotted spoon and add to the bowl of very cold water to stop the cooking. Drain, pat dry with paper towels and place the seafood in a large salad bowl.

Add the diced tomatoes, onions and basil. Season with salt and pepper. In a small bowl, combine the garlic with the oil and the lemon juice, mix well, then pour over seafood. Mix gently. Taste and adjust the seasoning and serve with slices of Italian bread.

HOT ANCHOVY DIP

Bagna Caôda

This classic Piedmont dish is typical of the region's robust cuisine.

⸢⸣ MAKES 4 SERVINGS

2 fennel bulbs	¼ cup butter
2 celery hearts	¾ cup olive oil
2 large, red or green sweet peppers	6 garlic cloves, finely chopped
1 or 2 bunches radishes, trimmed	8 flat anchovy fillets, chopped
½ pound small asparagus	Salt and freshly ground pepper, optional

Cut off long stalks and bruised leaves from fennels. Slice ends off bulbous bases. Wash and dry fennels. Cut into quarters, then horizontally into thick slices. Wash and dry celery hearts, peppers, radishes and asparagus. Slice celery hearts in half lengthwise. Slice peppers into quarters and remove seeds. Cut off tough asparagus ends. Using a sharp knife or potato peeler, peel outer skin. Arrange vegetables on a large platter.

Melt butter with oil in a small earthenware pot or small saucepan. When butter foams, add garlic. Sauté over medium heat until garlic begins to color; add anchovies. Reduce heat to very low. Stir until anchovies have almost dissolved. Season sparingly with salt and pepper, if desired. Keep dip warm at the table over a burner or on a warming tray. Serve with prepared vegetables.

Variation

Vegetables with Olive Oil Dip (*Verdure in Pinzimonio*): Prepare fresh vegetables. Combine 1 cup olive oil, 2 tablespoons salt and pepper to taste in a small bowl. Spoon dressing into 4 small bowls and place at each table setting.

ROASTED PEPPERS

Peperoni Arrostiti

MAKES 6 TO 8 SERVINGS

8 medium, red, yellow or green sweet peppers	3 tablespoons chopped parsley or fresh basil
½ cup olive oil	4 garlic cloves, finely chopped
6 flat anchovy fillets, mashed	Salt and freshly ground pepper to taste

Roast peppers over an open flame or under the broiler until skin is dark brown and blistered. Place peppers in a large plastic or brown paper bag and set aside 5 to 10 minutes. Peel peppers. Cut in half and remove pith and seeds. Cut peeled peppers into large strips. Pat dry with paper towels. Arrange peppers slightly overlapping on a medium platter.

In a small bowl, combine oil, anchovies, parsley or basil, garlic and salt and pepper. Taste and adjust for seasoning. Spoon anchovy dressing over peppers. Refrigerate several hours or overnight. Serve at room temperature.

GRILLED SHRIMP WRAPPED IN PROSCIUTTO

Scampi al Prosciutto di Parma

Fresh shrimp and good Italian prosciutto in a mouthwatering combination. Great for an appetizer or an entree.

MAKES 6 TO 8 SERVINGS

1½ pounds medium shrimp	½ cup dry unflavored bread crumbs mixed with 2 tablespoons chopped fresh parsley
¼ pound thinly sliced prosciutto	
¼ cup olive oil mixed with juice of 1 lemon	Lemon wedges

Preheat grill or broiler. Shell and devein the shrimp. Cut the prosciutto slices into 1-inch-wide and 2½-inch-long strips. Roll the prosciutto around shrimp. Thread wrapped shrimp onto 4 long metal skewers. Brush shrimp with the olive oil mixture and sprinkle them lightly with the bread crumb mixture. Put the skewers over the hot grill or under the broiler and cook about 1½ minutes or until golden. Turn skewers over and cook other side 1½ minutes or until golden. Serve hot with lemon wedges.

VEAL CARPACCIO
Carpaccio di Vitello

Veal carpaccio is more delicate than its beef counterpart. It is the perfect way to begin a multi-course meal.

§ **MAKES 6 TO 8 SERVINGS**

1 pound veal eye of round
4 to 5 tablespoons olive oil, preferably
    extra-virgin olive oil
Juice of 2 lemons
Salt and freshly ground pepper to taste

8 green onions, minced (white part only)
3 tablespoons capers, rinsed
3 to 4 ounces Parmesan cheese, cut into
    thin slivers

Freeze the meat for about 1 hour to make it easier to slice. Cut the meat into very thin slices. Put the slices between 2 sheets of plastic wrap and pound them lightly until they are almost transparent. Arrange the slices on individual dishes and sprinkle with oil and lemon juice. Season lightly with salt and pepper. Top with onions, capers and Parmesan cheese, and serve.

Soups

Soup is not the first item that comes to mind when you think about Italian food, but Italy has an outstanding selection of soups. Unfortunately, they have been upstaged by pasta both at home and abroad. Soup is always the first course, and it is into the first course that Italians have poured their hearts and traditions. The one Italian soup that non-Italians are familiar with is *Minestrone*. All too often this turns out to be a watery soup with pieces of vegetables and a few beans swimming about aimlessly in too much liquid. A soup in Italy takes on the characteristics of the region it comes from and embodies its traditions.

When I was growing up in Bologna, there was never any question of how to serve *tortellini*. In the classic Bolognese tradition, tortellini were always served in a rich broth. But today most people associate tortellini only with a cream sauce. Although Emilia-Romagna is the home of the very best *lasagne*, *tortellini* and *tagliatelle*, the traditional Sunday dinner in my family was always soup. The aroma of simmering broth filled the house by 8 A.M. Each Sunday a different kind of pasta would be cooked in the broth.

In some regions, soups are even more popular than pasta. Veneto, for example, boasts some of the best soups in Italy. Thick vegetable and bean soups are especially notable. Italian soups can be delicate and elegant. The lentil and bean soups, on the other hand, are substantial and filling. All these soups have one thing in common: a good broth. To produce a good soup, one must first produce a good broth. Broth is also a very important ingredient in other kinds of Italian cooking. With a good broth you can produce a sensational soup or add to meat juices to make a flavorful sauce. A good broth is also a key ingredient when making a perfect *risotto*.

In this chapter you will find recipes for a basic meat and chicken broth. Meat Broth is easy and inexpensive to make and can be used for soups and other cooking. Chicken Broth makes a good base for light soups and is ideal for risotto. Mixed Boiled Meats, page 161, produces an especially good broth because of the quality of meats used.

For a fine broth, remember these basic rules: Cooking should be done over very low heat. The broth should not boil, but should simmer very gently for 2½ to 3½ hours. This allows all the goodness and flavor of the meat and bones to be extracted. During the first few minutes of cooking, the surface foam should be skimmed off frequently. Seasoning should be done at the end because the liquid will reduce during cooking, concentrating the flavor.

We all have childhood memories that give us comfort and happiness. To me it is the memory of my mother in the kitchen preparing the Sunday dinner. Her soup would bring a glow to everyone's cheeks and fill us with a feeling of well-being.

Good food is a labor of love. How lucky we are not only to receive it but also to pass it on to our family and friends.

MEAT BROTH

Brodo di Carne

Keep a supply of this delicious broth in your freezer for soups and other cooking.

◊ MAKES ABOUT 2 QUARTS

2 pounds veal shanks, bones and scraps

2 pounds beef scraps and bones, preferably from knuckles

1 pound chicken bones and scraps

2 small carrots, peeled and cut into pieces

1 large celery stalk, cut into pieces

1 medium onion, peeled and quartered

A few sprigs of fresh parsley

2 small ripe tomatoes

Salt to taste

Wash bones, meat scraps and vegetables thoroughly under cold running water. Put all ingredients, except salt, in a large stockpot and cover with 3 to 4 inches of cold water. Cover pot partially, and bring liquid to a gentle boil over medium heat. As soon as water begins to bubble, reduce heat to low and skim off all foam that rises to surface of the water. Cook, barely simmering, about 3 hours. Season with salt only during last few minutes of cooking, because broth reduces considerably and its flavor becomes more accentuated.

If you are planning to use broth within a few hours, strain it through a fine-mesh strainer directly into another pot, and remove fat that comes to surface of broth with a spoon, or by dragging a piece of paper towel over broth surface. If broth is for later use, strain it into several small containers and place containers in a basin of iced water to cool completely. It can be kept in refrigerator, tightly covered, 2 to 3 days. Before using, remove fat that has solidified on surface. The broth is now fat free and ready to use or to freeze. Bring broth to a full boil before using.

Tip

Freezing broth for later use will give you the advantage of having flavorful broth at hand. Freeze it in small containers, or in ice-cube trays. When broth is frozen, unmold cubes, transfer to several plastic bags and freeze again until you are ready to use them.

CHICKEN BROTH

Brodo di Gallina

In Italy, hens are used to give the broth a distinct flavor.

⁀ MAKES 2 TO 2½ QUARTS

1 (2- to 3-pound) hen	2 medium tomatoes, chopped, or
1 to 1½ pounds chicken bones and scraps	1 tablespoon tomato paste
2 celery stalks, chopped	4 quarts water
1 medium onion, sliced	1 tablespoon salt

Place all ingredients except salt in a large stockpot. Cover and bring to a boil. Reduce heat to very low. Simmer covered 1 to 1½ hours, skimming surface foam occasionally with a slotted spoon. Add salt. Strain broth and use. Cool broth completely before freezing.

VEGETABLE BROTH

Brodo Vegetale

A flavorful vegetable broth can be used as an alternative to traditional meat and chicken broths. Its light quality is perfect for vegetable risotti and for spring and summer vegetable soups. This is a broth that takes no effort to prepare because it can be done with the most basic vegetables. Make a large batch and freeze it in ice-cube trays. Divide ice cubes into small containers or freezer bags and use as needed.

MAKES ABOUT 2 QUARTS

3 carrots

3 celery stalks

2 medium zucchini

2 tomatoes

1 large onion

10 cups water

Salt to taste

Wash vegetables, peel onion and cut the vegetables into small pieces. Add vegetables to a medium pot with water and place on medium heat. When water begins to boil, reduce heat to low and simmer uncovered about 1 hour. Season with salt.

Line a wire strainer with paper towels and strain broth, a few ladles at a time, directly into a large bowl. If you are not planning to use broth right away, cool it to room temperature. It can then be refrigerated for a few days or it can be frozen. Use it as instructed in individual recipes.

PASTINA AND PEAS IN CLEAR BROTH

Pastina e Piselli in Brodo

In Italy a good soup always has, as a base, a good broth. A nice bowl of steaming, flavorful broth with pastina (small pasta) added to it becomes a delightful comforting meal. This is one of the types of soups my mother would prepare for my brother, sister and me, when we were children. And it is the same type of soup I used to prepare for my daughters.

MAKES 6 SERVINGS

6 cups Meat Broth, page 22, or Chicken
    Broth, page 23
4 ounces pastina, such as bow ties or
    quadrucci, or rice

1½ pounds fresh peas in their pods,
    shelled, or 1 cup frozen peas, thawed
⅓ cup freshly grated Parmigiano-
    Reggiano cheese

Bring broth to a boil in a medium pot over high heat. Add pastina and fresh peas if using, and when broth comes back to boil, reduce heat to medium and cook, uncovered, until pastina and peas are tender, 3 to 5 minutes. (If using thawed peas instead of fresh, add them to soup during last minute of cooking.)

Ladle soup into individual soup bowls and serve hot with a generous sprinkle of freshly grated Parmigiano.

Variations

My father would enrich this type of light fragrant soup with a few beaten eggs stirred into simmering broth during its last few minutes of cooking. When eggs began to solidify and form little strands, he would turn the heat off, ladle the soup into his bowl and top generously with Parmigiano.

Tagliolini in Broth is a classic dish of Emilia-Romagna, Lombardy and Piedmont. Simply bring broth to a full boil and drop in 6 ounces of homemade or store-bought tagliolini. Reduce heat to medium and cook until pasta is tender. Serve with freshly grated Parmigiano-Reggiano.

BEANS, CLAMS AND MALTAGLIATI SOUP

Zuppa di Fagioli, Vongole e Maltagliati

This wonderful fragrant soup, which pairs beans, shellfish and pasta, is typical of many parts of Southern Italy.

§ə **MAKES 6 SERVINGS**

2 cups dried borlotti or cranberry beans, soaked overnight in cold water to cover generously

2 quarts (8 cups) cold water

2 to 2½ pounds clams, smallest you can get

⅓ cup extra-virgin olive oil plus additional to drizzle over soup

½ cup finely minced yellow onion

⅓ cup finely minced carrot

¼ cup mixed, finely chopped fresh herbs (parsley, sage, rosemary, mint, marjoram)

2 garlic cloves, finely minced

2 cups canned Italian plum tomatoes with their juices, put through a food mill to remove seeds

5 ounces dried small tubular pasta, such as ditalini or small bow ties

Drain and rinse beans under cold running water. Put them in a large pot, add water and place on high heat. As soon as water comes to a boil, reduce heat to low and simmer uncovered, stirring occasionally, until beans are tender, 45 minutes to 1 hour.

In a food processor, puree about half of beans with a ladle of their cooking water until smooth, and return to pot. Season lightly with salt and pepper and set aside until ready to use.

Soak clams in cold, salted water 20 minutes to purge them, then wash and scrub them well under cold running water. Discard any clams that are broken or already open and won't close when you touch them. Put clams in a large skillet with ½ cup water. Cover skillet and cook over high heat until clams open. Remove them with a slotted spoon to a bowl as they open. Discard any clams that do not open. Bring clam cooking juices back to a boil and cook until liquid is reduced by about half. Strain liquid into a small bowl and set aside.

Heat oil in a small saucepan over medium heat. Add onion and carrot. Cook, stirring, until vegetables are light golden and soft, about 6 minutes. Add herbs and garlic and cook, stirring, 1 to 2 minutes. Add reserved clam liquid and tomatoes. Season with salt and pepper. As soon as sauce begins to bubble, reduce heat to medium-low and simmer, uncovered, until sauce is reduced by about half, about 10 minutes. Add clams to sauce and cook, stirring, 1 to 2 minutes. Add tomatoes to pot with beans and turn heat to medium-low. Simmer uncovered 4 to 5 minutes.

Meanwhile bring a medium pot of water to a boil. Add a pinch of salt and pasta. Cook uncovered over high heat until pasta is tender but still a bit firm to bite. Drain pasta and add it to soup. Turn heat off under pot and allow soup to rest 10 to 15 minutes. Serve with a light drizzle of olive oil.

Variations

If you prefer soup without pasta, you might want to slightly increase amount of clams. Mussels can also be used.

PARMESAN CHEESE, BREAD CRUMB AND NUTMEG SOUP

Passatelli in Brodo

This is a delicious and unique soup from the Emilia-Romagna region.

✿ MAKES 6 TO 8 SERVINGS

10 to 12 cups broth from Mixed Boiled Meats, page 161, or Meat Broth, page 22	½ cup fine, dry unflavored bread crumbs
	½ teaspoon freshly grated nutmeg
	2 large eggs
¾ cup freshly grated Parmesan cheese	Additional Parmesan cheese

Prepare Meat Broth.

On a pastry board or in a large bowl, combine ¾ cup Parmesan cheese, bread crumbs and nutmeg. Mix well. Add eggs. Mix ingredients thoroughly and work into a ball. Dough should be smooth and pliable.

Bring broth to a boil in a large saucepan. Put dough into a ricer or food mill and rice directly into broth. Reduce heat. Simmer 1 to 2 minutes. Serve hot with Parmesan cheese.

BARLEY, POTATOES AND STRING BEAN SOUP

Zuppa di Orzo, Patate e Fagiolini

There was a time when everyone in Italy made soups. Thick, delicious soups were prepared in winter months, while lighter soups were favored during hot days. Today there seems to be less time to devote to this type of cooking. This thick soup, which has a savory base of onion, carrot, parsley and pancetta, tastes even better the day after. It can be served hot, or at room temperature.

MAKES 10 SERVINGS

2 tablespoons butter

2 to 3 tablespoons extra-virgin olive oil

1 cup finely minced yellow onion

½ cup finely minced carrot

2 to 3 tablespoons chopped flat-leaf Italian parsley

1 thick slice (¼ pound) pancetta, finely minced or chopped

1 cup (about ½ pound) husked, polished pearl barley, washed in several changes of cold water

2 medium boiling potatoes, peeled and diced into small pieces

2½ quarts Meat Broth, page 22, low-sodium canned beef broth or water

¼ pound string beans, ends removed, washed and cut into 1-inch pieces

⅓ to ½ cup freshly grated Parmigiano-Reggiano cheese

Heat butter and oil in a large pot over medium heat. Add onion, carrot and parsley and cook, stirring, until vegetables are soft, 6 to 7 minutes. Add pancetta and cook, stirring, 2 to 3 minutes longer, or until it is light golden. Add barley and potatoes, stir 1 to 2 minutes, then add broth. Season with salt. As soon as broth comes to a boil, reduce heat to low and partially cover pot. Simmer, stirring occasionally, about 30 minutes.

Add beans and cook until beans, barley and potatoes are tender, 10 to 15 minutes. Taste, adjust seasoning and turn heat off under pot. Let soup rest about 10 minutes or so before serving with Parmigiano.

LENTIL SOUP

Zuppa di Lenticchie

The flavor of this nutritious soup improves if made one or two days ahead.

MAKES 8 TO 10 SERVINGS

2 cups lentils	¼ cup olive oil
4 cups Meat Broth, page 22, or 3 cups canned beef broth	1 medium onion, finely chopped
6 to 8 cups water	2 tablespoons chopped parsley
2 celery stalks, finely chopped	2 garlic cloves, chopped
2 carrots, finely chopped	¼ pound pancetta, page 4 chopped
1 cup canned crushed Italian-style or whole tomatoes	Salt and freshly ground pepper to taste
	8 to 10 thick slices Italian bread
	1 cup freshly grated Parmesan cheese

Place lentils in a large bowl. Add enough cold water to cover and let stand overnight. Discard any lentils that float to the surface. Drain and rinse lentils thoroughly.

Prepare Meat Broth. Place lentils in a large saucepan. Add water, broth, celery and carrots. Cover and bring to a boil. Reduce heat. Simmer 50 to 60 minutes, stirring occasionally. Press tomatoes through a food mill or sieve to remove seeds. Heat oil in a small saucepan. Add onion, parsley and garlic. Sauté over medium heat 2 to 3 minutes.

Add pancetta. Sauté 2 to 3 minutes or until pancetta is lightly browned. Add tomato pulp. Season with salt and pepper. Reduce heat. Cook uncovered 15 to 20 minutes. With a slotted spoon, place a third of lentil mixture in a blender or food processor. Process until smooth. Return to saucepan. Add tomato mixture. Simmer uncovered 10 minutes. Taste and adjust for seasoning.

Toast bread until golden on both sides. Place 1 slice toasted bread in each soup bowl. Sprinkle generously with Parmesan cheese. Ladle soup into bowls. Serve hot or at room temperature.

VEGETABLE SOUP

Minestrone di Verdura

There are as many versions of vegetable soup in Italy as there are cooks.

◊ MAKES 8 TO 10 SERVINGS

8 cups Chicken Broth, page 23, or
    4 cups canned chicken broth and
    4 cups water
⅓ cup olive oil
¼ cup chopped parsley
4 garlic cloves, chopped
¼ pound pancetta, page 4, finely
    chopped
3 cups shredded cabbage
1 medium onion, finely chopped
2 carrots, finely chopped

1 celery stalk, finely chopped
1 potato, peeled, finely chopped
2 zucchini, finely chopped
1 large tomato, chopped
¼ pound mushrooms, finely chopped
¼ pound string beans, finely chopped
3 or 4 pieces prosciutto rind, page 5, or 1
    smoked ham shank
Salt and freshly ground pepper to taste
½ cup freshly grated Parmesan cheese

Prepare Chicken Broth.

Heat oil in a large saucepan. Add parsley and garlic. Sauté over medium heat. Before garlic changes color, add pancetta. Sauté until lightly browned. Stir in cabbage. Cover and cook 1 to 2 minutes. Add remaining vegetables to saucepan. Cover and cook about 5 minutes.

Add broth and water, if using, and prosciutto rind or ham shank. Cover and reduce heat. Simmer 40 to 50 minutes. Remove half the vegetables with a slotted spoon. Place in a blender or food processor and process until smooth. Return to saucepan. Season with salt and pepper. Serve hot with Parmesan cheese.

Variation

Toast about 20 thick slices Italian bread. Place 2 slices in each soup bowl and sprinkle generously with Parmesan cheese. Ladle soup into bowls. Serve with additional Parmesan cheese.

Tip

You can transform a vegetable soup into a cream of vegetable soup. Puree the vegetables in a food processor or blender and stir in some cream.

RICE AND PEA SOUP

Risi e Bisi

A classic Venetian soup, it should be thick enough to eat with a fork.

☙ MAKES 6 TO 8 SERVINGS

8 cups Meat Broth, page 22

¼ cup butter

1 tablespoon olive oil

1 small onion, chopped

¼ pound pancetta, page 4, chopped

2 tablespoons chopped parsley

2½ cups fresh peas or frozen peas, thawed

2 cups arborio rice, page 5

⅓ cup freshly grated Parmesan cheese plus additional for serving

Prepare Meat Broth.

Melt 2 tablespoons butter with oil in a medium saucepan. When butter foams, add onion, pancetta and parsley. Sauté over medium heat until pancetta is lightly browned. Add peas and ⅓ cup broth. Cook 2 to 3 minutes; set aside.

Bring remaining broth to a boil in a large saucepan. Add rice. Cook uncovered over high heat 8 to 10 minutes, stirring occasionally. Add onion mixture. Cook 10 to 15 minutes or until rice is tender but firm to the bite. Stir in remaining butter and ⅓ cup Parmesan cheese. Serve hot with additional Parmesan cheese.

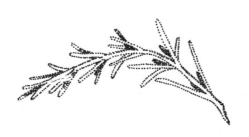

MY MOTHER'S BEAN SOUP

Zuppa di Fagioli alla Maniera di mia Madre

There are certain childhood dishes that cannot be forgotten. For me, this hearty soup is one of them.

MAKES 8 TO 10 SERVINGS

2 cups dried pinto beans

4 cups Meat Broth, page 22, or 3 cups
    canned beef broth

6 to 8 cups water

1 large potato, peeled, halved

1 carrot, halved

1 celery stalk, halved

2 to 3 slices prosciutto rind, page 4, or
    salt pork

1 cup canned crushed Italian-style or
    whole tomatoes

¼ cup olive oil

3 tablespoons chopped parsley

2 garlic cloves, chopped

1 small onion, chopped

¼ pound pancetta, page 4, chopped

Salt and freshly ground pepper to taste

8 to 10 thick slices Italian bread

1 cup freshly grated Parmesan cheese

Place beans in a large bowl. Add enough cold water to cover and let stand overnight. Drain and rinse beans thoroughly.

Prepare Meat Broth. Place beans in a large saucepan. Add water, broth, potato, carrot, celery and prosciutto rind or salt pork. Cover and bring to a boil. Reduce heat. Simmer 50 to 60 minutes, stirring occasionally.

Press tomatoes through a food mill or sieve to remove seeds. Heat oil in a medium saucepan. Add parsley, garlic and onion. Sauté over medium heat 2 to 3 minutes. Add pancetta. Sauté until pancetta is lightly browned. Stir in tomato pulp and season with salt and pepper. Reduce heat. Cook uncovered 15 to 20 minutes.

With a slotted spoon, place potato, carrot, celery and half the beans in a blender or food processor. Process until smooth. Return to saucepan. Add tomato mixture. Simmer uncovered 10 minutes. Taste and adjust for seasoning.

Toast bread until golden on both sides. Place 1 slice toasted bread in each soup bowl. Sprinkle generously with Parmesan cheese. Ladle soup into bowls.

BEAN SOUP VENETO STYLE

Pasta e Fagioli alla Veneta

The Veneto region is famous for its marvelous bean soups.

§● MAKES 8 TO 10 SERVINGS

2 cups dried pinto beans

4 cups Meat Broth, page 22 or 3 cups
    canned beef broth

6 to 8 cups water

6 tablespoons olive oil

2 slices prosciutto rind, page 4, or salt
    pork

1 carrot, chopped

1 celery stalk, chopped

1 medium onion, chopped

1 sprig fresh rosemary or 1 teaspoon
    dried rosemary

2 tablespoons chopped parsley

2 garlic cloves, chopped

1 tablespoon all-purpose flour

2 tablespoons tomato paste

Salt and freshly ground pepper to taste

¼ pound small elbow macaroni, ditalini
    or arborio rice, page 5

⅓ cup freshly grated Parmesan cheese
    plus additional for serving

Place beans in a large bowl. Add enough cold water to cover and let stand overnight. Drain and rinse beans thoroughly.

Prepare Meat Broth. Place beans in a large saucepan. Add water, broth, 2 tablespoons oil, prosciutto rind or salt pork, carrot, celery and onion. Cover and bring to a boil. Reduce heat. Simmer 50 to 60 minutes, stirring occasionally.

Heat 3 tablespoons oil in a small saucepan. Add rosemary. Cook over medium heat until lightly browned. Discard rosemary. Add parsley and garlic; sauté. When garlic changes color, stir in flour. Cook and stir about 1 minute. Remove 1 cup cooking liquid from bean mixture. Stir in tomato paste. Stir into flour mixture. Season with salt and pepper. Cook 5 to 10 minutes, stirring frequently. Add to bean mixture.

With a slotted spoon, place a third of bean mixture in a blender or food processor. Process until smooth. Return to saucepan. Bring soup to a boil. Add pasta or rice and cook over high heat 8 to 10 minutes. Stir several times during cooking. Taste and adjust for seasoning. Stir 1 tablespoon oil and ⅓ cup Parmesan cheese into soup. Serve hot with additional Parmesan cheese.

CREAM OF POTATO AND LEEK SOUP

Crema di Patate e Porri

Leeks are closely related to onions but have a flavor all their own.

MAKES 6 SERVINGS

6 to 8 cups Meat Broth, page 22

2 pounds potatoes

1 pound leeks

2 egg yolks

½ cup whipping cream

1 tablespoon chopped parsley

Salt and freshly ground pepper to taste

½ cup freshly grated Parmesan cheese

Toasted bread

Prepare Meat Broth.

Peel and chop potatoes. Trim ends and tough outside leaves from leeks. Cut leeks lengthwise through to center. Wash under cold running water, pulling layers apart so grit is removed. Slice into rounds. Put potatoes and leeks into a medium saucepan. Add enough broth to cover. Cook uncovered over medium heat until vegetables are tender.

With a slotted spoon, place vegetables in a blender or food processor. Process until smooth. Return puree to broth. Bring mixture to a boil. Remove from heat. Beat together egg yolks and cream in a small bowl. Quickly beat egg yolk mixture into hot soup. Stir in parsley. Season with salt and pepper. Serve hot with Parmesan cheese and toasted bread.

ONION SOUP ITALIAN STYLE

Zuppa di Cipolle all'Italiana

Homemade Meat Broth and top-quality Parmesan cheese are vital to the success of this soup.

❧ MAKES 6 SERVINGS

10 to 12 cups Meat Broth, page 22
6 tablespoons butter
8 large onions, thinly sliced
⅓ cup brandy

½ cup all-purpose flour
12 thick slices Italian bread
1 to 1½ cups freshly grated Parmesan
  cheese

Prepare Meat Broth. Simmer broth in a large saucepan.

Melt butter in another large saucepan. When butter foams, add onions. Sauté over medium heat until pale yellow. Stir in brandy. When brandy is three-quarters evaporated, stir in flour. Reduce heat to medium-low. Cook 1 to 2 minutes, stirring constantly. Gradually stir in hot broth. Season with salt and pepper. Cover and simmer 30 to 40 minutes.

Preheat oven to 350F (175C). Toast bread until golden on both sides. Place 2 slices toasted bread in each of 6 ovenproof soup bowls. Add 1 to 2 tablespoons Parmesan cheese. Ladle soup into bowls. Sprinkle each serving with a generous tablespoon Parmesan cheese. Bake 10 to 12 minutes. Place briefly under preheated broiler for a golden crust. Serve immediately.

Pasta

Pasta, which has been basic to the Italian diet for centuries, is synonymous with Italy. Of course pasta is also indigenous to other countries, but nowhere in the world is the image of pasta as exciting, tempting and glorious as it is in Italy. Pasta is undoubtedly Italy's greatest culinary asset.

I was born and raised in Bologna, a city famous for its superlative fresh pasta, and was fed a daily dose of tagliatelle, tagliolini, cappelletti, tortellini and lasagne. My mother, a superlative cook, would prepare her daily homemade pasta with the speed of sound. She would put the flour on the wooden board, make a well in the center and crack the eggs into the well. Then, with fast, experienced hands, she would mix eggs and flour and in no time at all she would produce a beautiful, soft yellow dough. She would roll the dough out with a long rolling pin into a large circular, transparent sheet, then she would cut the sheet into the chosen shape. It was a miracle, or so I thought, that with a bunch of flour and only a few eggs, something so incredibly delicious could be accomplished. By the time I was fifteen, I too knew how to make pasta by hand, even though mine lacked the silkiness and smoothness of my mother's pasta.

On occasions we were served a dish of factory-made pasta, such as spaghetti or maccheroni, which my father would barely tolerate, having been fed all his life the homemade product. Today, he would be shocked to know that 55 million Italians use factory-made pasta on a daily basis, even in the north, since the majority of the women work outside the home and have much less time to devote to pasta making.

In this country, the image of pasta has changed drastically in the last ten years. Once a poor man's staple, pasta has become today a very "in" food. Now that nutritionists have told us we should eat more pasta, much emphasis is spent on learning the art of pasta making. Pasta is a highly satisfying food. It is comfort food at its best. Colorful, ebullient, assertive or delicate, a few ounces of pasta with a moderate amount of sauce can generally satisfy hunger and leave you in a happy, satisfied mood. We can finally indulge in a diet of pasta, without too much guilt.

Homemade pasta and factory-made pasta are two completely different products, both delicious in their own way. Homemade pasta, which uses white, unbleached all-purpose flour, is light and delicate, perfect for stuffed preparations, such as ravioli, tortellini, lasagne, tagliatelle and tagliolini. The sauces for homemade pasta are somewhat refined, light and mildly seasoned. Factory-made pasta, which is made with durum wheat flour (semolina), comes in a myriad of shapes, such as spaghetti, linguine, penne, shells and rigatoni. It is best suited for more assertive, ebullient and colorful sauces and is a favorite of Southern Italians.

Faithful to the Northern Italian tradition, most of the pasta in this chapter is homemade. You will find the "Classic Method for Making Pasta Dough" rolled out with a rolling pin, on page 42, as well as the "Basic Egg Pasta Dough" rolled out with a hand-cranked pasta machine, on page 40.

Ingredients

Use unbleached all-purpose flour. This flour has a moderate amount of gluten, which will make the dough soft and pliable. Semolina flour (durum wheat flour) is almost never used in Northern Italy to make homemade pasta. Semolina flour is used for factory-made pasta.

Use large eggs brought to room temperature. If you can find eggs with a really orange yolk, your pasta will have the golden color that egg pasta should have. In Tuscany a drop of oil and a pinch of salt are added to the dough. In all the other Northern Italian regions, only flour and eggs are used.

Equipment Needed to Make Pasta Dough by Hand

The best surface for kneading pasta is wood. The warmth and grain of wood will give your pasta a special texture. Formica or marble can also be used. A dough or pastry scraper will clean the sticky pieces of dough attached to the board.

Use a fork to mix the flour with the eggs.

Equipment Needed to Roll Out Pasta Dough

If you are planning to roll out pasta dough by hand, a long Italian rolling pin, 32 inches long and 1½ inches in diameter, would be ideal. If your local gourmet cooking store does not carry it, use a regular rolling pin.

If you are planning to roll out the pasta dough by machine, look for a little hand-cranked pasta machine, which can be found in most department stores at a very reasonable price. The main part of the pasta machine is for kneading and rolling the dough through its two steel rollers. This machine comes with two attachments to cut the sheet of dough into wide and thin noodles.

Cutting, Storing and Cooking Noodles

After you have made your pasta and rolled it out by hand, page 42, or by machine, page 41, you need to dry the pasta sheets 8 to 12 minutes, depending on the heat of your room. When the pasta is no longer sticky, put it through the cutting blades of the pasta machine, according to the width you wish to make. Arrange noodles in soft bundles on a wooden board or a tablecloth. They can be cooked immediately or they can be allowed to dry and cooked later on. If you plan to store the noodles, let them dry at least 24 hours. At this point the noodles are brittle. Place them gently in plastic bags or in a plastic container. Seal tightly and store at room temperature. They will keep well for two to three weeks.

To cook fresh noodles, follow these simple, basic rules.

- Use 4 to 5 quarts of water for 1 pound of pasta.

- Bring the water to a boil. Add salt and pasta. Cover the pot and bring the water back to a boil, then remove the lid. Stir a few times during cooking.

- The cooking of the noodles will depend on their freshness. Freshly made noodles will cook quickly. The longer they dry, the longer they need to cook.

- Never overcook pasta. It should always be firm to the bite.

- Never rinse pasta, unless specifically indicated in a recipe.

- Never precook pasta unless you are making lasagne or cannelloni.

Cutting, Storing and Cooking Stuffed Pasta

For stuffed pasta, such as tortellini and agnolotti, each sheet of dough must be cut and stuffed *immediately* so the moistness of the dough can give a tight seal. Stuffed pasta should not be made more than one day ahead of cooking time. Many stuffings are very moist and if left to stand will make the dough sticky. Specific instructions on cutting and stuffing are given with the recipes. The principle for cooking stuffed pasta is the same as that for noodles. The fresher the pasta the shorter the cooking time.

Factory-Made Pasta

Factory-made pasta comes in myriads of shapes and sizes. Years ago the only factory-made pasta available in this country were spaghetti, linguine and macaroni. Today we have many choices. Good factory-made pasta, imported from Italy and made with 100 percent semolina flour, is available all over the country. This pasta has the gold coloring of wheat and when properly cooked, it almost doubles in volume. The cooking time of dried pasta varies depending on the size, shape and brand you choose. Read the instructions on the label and taste it as it cooks. Leave the pasta slightly undercooked, so by the time you toss it with the sauce and bring it to the table, it will be simply perfect.

BASIC EGG PASTA DOUGH

Pasta all'Uovo

Altitude, humidity and the size of the eggs will influence the amount of flour needed to make pasta.

	TO MAKE		
USE THESE INGREDIENTS	3 to 4 servings	5 to 6 servings	7 to 8 servings
All-purpose flour	2¼ cups	3 cups	4½ cups
Eggs	3	4	6

Put flour on a pastry board and make a well in the center. Break eggs into well; beat with a fork. Draw some flour from inner rim of well over eggs, beating constantly. Keep adding flour a little at a time until you have a soft dough. Put dough aside.

With a pastry scraper, remove bits and pieces of dough attached to board. Lightly flour board and your hands. Knead dough 10 to 12 minutes, adding flour a little at a time until dough is smooth and pliable. Insert a finger into center of dough. If it comes out almost dry, dough is ready for pasta machine. If dough is sticky, knead it a little longer adding more flour.

Set rollers of pasta machine at their widest opening. Cut an egg-size piece from dough. Wrap remaining dough in a cloth towel to prevent it from drying. Flatten small piece of dough, dust with flour and fold in half. Run it through pasta machine. Repeat this step 5 to 8 times or until dough is smooth and not sticky. Change notch of pasta machine to the next setting and run dough through once without folding it. Keep changing setting and working pasta sheet through machine until pasta reaches desired thickness. A good thickness for general use is about $\frac{1}{16}$ inch. Sprinkle dough with flour between rollings if it is sticky.

BASIC SPINACH PASTA DOUGH

Pasta Verde

Once you have tasted homemade pasta, no substitute will do!

	TO MAKE		
USE THESE INGREDIENTS	3 to 4 servings	5 to 6 servings	7 to 8 servings
Frozen spinach	$\frac{1}{3}$ (10-ounce) pkg.	$\frac{1}{2}$ (10-ounce) pkg.	$\frac{2}{3}$ (10-ounce) pkg.
All-purpose flour	2 cups	3 cups	4 cups
Eggs	2	2	4

Cook spinach according to package instructions. Drain thoroughly. Squeeze spinach to remove as much moisture as possible. Chop spinach very fine. Put flour on a pastry board and make a well in the center. Break eggs into well; beat with a fork. Add chopped spinach and beat to combine. Continue as for Basic Egg Pasta Dough, page 40.

Classic Method for Making Pasta Dough

Prepare dough as directed on page 40. Place dough on a lightly floured surface. Flatten ball of dough with a rolling pin or the palms of your hands. The ideal rolling pin should be 32 inches long and 1½ inches in diameter. Roll out dough, starting from center and moving toward edges. Rotate dough slightly and roll out again from center toward edges. Repeat several times. Dough should be rolled into a wide circle. Dust surface lightly if sticking. To roll out pasta to an even thinness, wrap the far edge of pasta sheet around rolling pin. Roll less than half of pasta sheet toward you. With the palms of your hands, gently press against center of rolling pin. Roll pin forward while the palms of your hands move toward ends of rolling pin. With this motion, pasta will be stretched forward as well as sideways. Rotate sheet of pasta slightly and repeat the motion. Dust lightly with flour if dough is sticky. Repeat this step until dough is thin and almost transparent. Try to work as quickly as possible to avoid dough drying.

For stuffed pasta, cut into desired shapes and stuff immediately. For noodles, let pasta circle dry on a wooden surface or tablecloth, 15 to 20 minutes. Fold pasta loosely into a flat roll, not wider than 3 inches. With a large sharp knife, cut pasta into desired width. Open out noodles. Place in soft bundles on a wooden surface or tablecloth. Dry noodles 10 to 15 minutes longer before cooking. Dry completely for 24 hours if you intend to store them.

PASTA WITH ALMONDS AND CREAM

Pasta con Mandorle e Panna

Almonds and cream are combined to make a simple dish with a delightful flavor.

§֍ MAKES 4 TO 6 SERVINGS

3 ounces blanched almonds	Salt and white pepper to taste
¼ cup butter	1 pound penne or pasta shells
2 garlic cloves, minced	8 to 10 fresh basil leaves, finely shredded
1 cup Chicken Broth, page 23, or canned	or 2 tablespoons chopped fresh parsley
chicken broth	½ cup freshly grated Parmesan cheese
2 cups whipping cream	

Preheat oven to 350F (175C). Put almonds on a baking sheet and bake until light golden.

Melt butter in a large skillet. When butter foams, add garlic and almonds. Cook over medium heat, stirring, until the garlic begins to color, less than 1 minute. Add broth and cream; season with salt and pepper. Cook, stirring, until the sauce is reduced almost by half and has a medium-thick consistency.

While the sauce is simmering, bring a large pot of salted water to a boil. Add the pasta and cook uncovered until the pasta is tender but firm to the bite, 7 to 8 minutes. Drain the pasta and add it to the sauce. Stir in the basil or the parsley and ¼ cup of Parmesan cheese. Mix quickly over very low heat until the pasta is well coated with the sauce, 20 to 30 seconds. Serve at once with remaining Parmesan cheese if you wish.

RODRIGO'S PENNE WITH PROSCIUTTO, PEAS AND CREAM

Le Penne di Rodrigo con Prosciutto, Piselli e Panna

One night at Rodrigo, one of my favorite restaurants of Bologna, I ordered a pasta dish that had a luscious sauce of prosciutto, peas and cream. The sauce, which barely coated the pasta, was very light and absolutely delicious, because cream had been kept to a minimum and a small amount of broth had been added in its place.

୨୭ **MAKES 4 TO 6 SERVINGS**

1 cup shelled fresh green peas or thawed
    frozen peas

3 tablespoons butter

⅓ cup very finely minced shallot or
    yellow onion

2 or 3 thick slices (¼ pound) prosciutto,
    cut into strips and diced

¾ cup heavy cream

½ cup Chicken Broth, page 23, or low-
    sodium canned

Salt to taste

1 pound penne or garganelli

⅓ to ½ cup freshly grated Parmigiano-
    Reggiano cheese

If using fresh peas, drop them into a small saucepan of salted boiling water, and cook until peas are tender but still a bit firm. Drain and set aside.

Melt butter in a large skillet over medium heat. When butter foams, add shallot or onion. Cook, stirring occasionally, until shallot is light golden and soft, about 5 minutes. Add prosciutto and stir 1 to 2 minutes. Add peas, stir once or twice, then add cream and broth. Season with salt. As soon as cream comes to a boil, reduce heat and let sauce bubble gently until it has a medium-thick consistency, 3 to 5 minutes. Taste, adjust seasoning and turn heat off.

Meanwhile, cook pasta, uncovered, in plenty of boiling salted water, until tender but still firm to the bite. Drain pasta and place in skillet with sauce. Add a small handful of Parmigiano and mix over medium heat until pasta and sauce are well combined. Add some more broth or cream if sauce seems a bit dry. Taste, adjust seasoning and serve with remaining Parmigiano.

BAKED PASTA WITH BOLOGNESE MEAT RAGÙ

Pasta al Forno con Ragù alla Bolognese

Some dishes, made with leftover sauces or meat ragùs, are even better the second time around. My mother would combine leftover Bolognese meat ragù with Salsa Balsamella (béchamel sauce or white sauce) and rigatoni or penne. She would dust them generously with Parmigiano and bake them until cheese melted and top of pasta was golden and crisp. The baking dish went from oven to table where pasta was spooned onto our plates.

❦ MAKES 6 SERVINGS

1 recipe Bolognese Meat Sauce, page 206	Pinch of salt
White Sauce	1 pound penne
1½ cups milk	½ cup freshly grated Parmigiano-
3 tablespoons unsalted butter	Reggiano cheese
2 tablespoons all-purpose flour	1 tablespoon butter

Prepare meat sauce and set aside until ready to use.

Prepare White Sauce as instructed on page 205, using proportions listed above.

Preheat oven to 400F (205C). Generously butter bottom and sides of a baking dish.

Bring a large pot of salted water to boil. Add pasta and cook uncovered over high heat until pasta is cooked only halfway through and has a firm consistency. Drain pasta and place in a large bowl.

Add 2½ cups of meat sauce, ⅔ cup of white sauce and about half of Parmigiano. Mix until pasta and sauces are well combined. Put pasta in prepared baking dish, sprinkle top with remaining Parmigiano and dot with butter. Place dish in middle rack of oven and bake until top has a nice golden color, 8 to 10 minutes. Remove dish from oven and let it settle a few minutes. Bring dish to table and serve.

GARGANELLI WITH DRIED PORCINI AND SMOKED HAM

Garganelli con Porcini e Prosciutto Affumicato

This is one of the delicious dishes of Trattoria Gigina in Bologna that departs a bit from tradition because speck, smoked Italian ham from the Alto Adige region, is used instead of prosciutto. Of course prosciutto or pancetta can also be used. And if you can get fresh porcini mushrooms, clean them with a damp cloth, slice them and use them instead of dry porcini, just as instructed below.

⁕ MAKES 4 TO 6 SERVINGS

1½ ounces dried porcini mushrooms, soaked in 2 cups lukewarm water 20 minutes

4 tablespoons butter

½ cup very finely minced yellow onion

2 or 3 thick slices (3 ounces) speck or prosciutto, finely diced

1 cup dry white wine

¼ cup heavy cream

Salt to taste

2 tablespoons chopped fresh flat-leaf Italian parsley

1 recipe Pasta Dough (page 40) rolled out and cut for garganelli or 1 pound imported dried garganelli or penne rigate

½ to ¾ cup freshly grated Parmigiano-Reggiano cheese

Drain porcini mushrooms and reserve soaking water. Rinse mushrooms well under cold running water and chop them roughly. Line a strainer with paper towels and strain mushroom water into a bowl to get rid of sandy deposits. Set aside.

Heat 3 tablespoons of the butter in a large skillet over medium heat. Add onion and cook, stirring, until onion is lightly golden and soft, about 5 minutes. Add porcini mushrooms and speck or prosciutto and stir for a minute or two. Add wine. Cook, stirring occasionally, until wine is reduced by about half. Add 1 cup of reserved porcini water and cream. Season lightly with salt. As soon as sauce begins to bubble, reduce heat to low and simmer, uncovered until it has a medium-thick consistency, 4 to 5 minutes. Stir parsley and remaining butter into sauce and turn heat off under skillet.

Meanwhile bring a large pot of water to a boil. Add 1 tablespoon of salt and pasta. Cook, uncovered, over high heat until pasta is tender but still a bit firm to the bite. Scoop up and reserve about 1 cup of pasta cooking water.

Drain pasta and place in skillet with sauce. Season lightly with salt, and add about ⅓ cup of Parmigiano. Toss everything quickly over medium heat until pasta and sauce are well combined.

If pasta seems dry, add some of reserved pasta water and stir quickly to incorporate. Taste, adjust seasoning and serve with remaining Parmigiano.

Variation

For a tomato-based sauce, stir 2 tablespoons imported double concentrated Italian tomato paste into 2 cups of reserved porcini water and add to mushrooms. Omit cream. Simmer sauce until it has a medium-thick consistency.

TAGLIOLINI WITH SOLE AND LEMON ZEST

I Tagliolini con Sugo di Sogliola e Limone

In this dish fresh sole is cubed and sautéed quickly in oil scented with garlic. Some wine, grated zest of lemon and fresh marjoram complete the sauce. This is a dish that is as light as it is quick to prepare, and relies on the freshness of the fish and marjoram.

MAKES 4 TO 6 SERVINGS

⅓ cup olive oil

2 garlic cloves, peeled

¾ pound (about ½ inch thick) filet of
    sole, diced

½ cup dry white wine

Grated zest of 1 lemon

Salt and freshly ground pepper to taste

1 tablespoon butter

⅓ cup loosely packed marjoram leaves
    or 1 to 2 tablespoons chopped fresh
    flat-leaf Italian parsley

1 recipe Pasta Dough, page 41, rolled out
    and cut for tagliolini, or 1 pound
    imported tagliolini

Heat oil in a large skillet over medium heat. Add garlic and cook until golden brown on all sides.

Discard garlic and add sole. Cook, stirring, until sole is light golden and fish juices have thickened, about 2 minutes. Increase heat to high and add wine. Stir until wine is almost all reduced. Add lemon zest, and season with salt and just a bit of pepper. Reduce heat to medium and cook, stirring occasionally, until liquid in skillet has a medium-thick consistency, 3 to 4 minutes. Add butter, marjoram or parsley, stir once or twice and turn heat off.

Meanwhile bring a large pot of water to a boil. Add 1 tablespoon of salt and pasta. Cook, uncovered, over high heat, until pasta is tender but still firm to the bite. Scoop up and reserve about 1 cup of pasta cooking water.

Drain pasta and add it to sauce. Stir quickly over medium heat until pasta and sauce are well combined. Add some of reserved pasta water if pasta seems a bit dry. Taste, adjust seasoning and serve.

PENNE WITH ONION, RED BELL PEPPERS AND TOMATOES

Penne alla Peperonata

In Italian home cooking, many vegetable dishes are versatile enough to become sauces for pasta. Here is a perfect example. Peperonata, a traditional Bolognese vegetable dish of slowly braised onion, bell peppers and tomatoes, becomes a terrific sauce for penne, rigatoni or shells. The addition of a bit of pancetta to the vegetables enlivens the dish with extra flavor.

MAKES 4 TO 6 SERVINGS

½ cup extra-virgin olive oil

1 thick slice (2 to 3 ounces) pancetta, diced, optional

1 medium yellow onion, thinly sliced

5 large red bell peppers, (about 2 pounds), cored, seeded and diced

1 pound firm, ripe tomatoes, seeded and diced

Salt and freshly ground black pepper

2 to 3 tablespoons balsamic vinegar, optional

1 pound penne rigate or shells

Heat ⅓ cup of oil in a large skillet over medium heat. Add pancetta, if using, and cook, stirring, until golden, 2 to 3 minutes. With a slotted spoon transfer pancetta to a plate.

Place skillet back on medium heat. Add onion, cook, stirring, 2 to 3 minutes then add peppers. Cook, stirring, until peppers begin to color and soften, 5 to 6 minutes. Return pancetta to skillet, add tomatoes and season with salt and pepper. Reduce heat to medium-low and cook uncovered, stirring occasionally, until peppers are tender and juices in skillet have thickened, 15 to 20 minutes. Add a little water or broth if juices should reduce too much. Taste and adjust seasoning and turn heat off. (Sauce can be prepared several hours or a day ahead and refrigerated. Reheat gently before using.) Makes 2½ to 3 cups sauce.

Cook pasta in plenty of salted boiling water until tender but still firm to bite. Put skillet back on medium heat. Add remaining oil and balsamic vinegar if using. Stir to blend.

Drain pasta and add to skillet with sauce. Season lightly with salt. Mix quickly over low heat until pasta and sauce are well combined. Taste, adjust seasoning and serve.

TAGLIATELLE BOLOGNA STYLE

Tagliatelle alla Bolognese

For a family meal follow this satisfying dish with some cheese and a green salad.

MAKES 6 SERVINGS

Basic Egg Pasta Dough, page 40, made with 3 cups all-purpose flour
2 cups Bolognese Meat Sauce, page 206
⅓ cup freshly grated Parmesan cheese plus additional for serving

Prepare noodles from Basic Egg Pasta Dough. Prepare Bolognese Meat Sauce and keep warm.

Fill a very large saucepan two-thirds full with salted water. Bring water to a boil. Add noodles. Bring water back to a boil and cook noodles uncovered until tender but firm to the bite. Drain noodles and place in a warm deep dish or bowl.

Add sauce and ⅓ cup Parmesan cheese. Toss gently until mixed. Serve immediately with additional Parmesan cheese.

GREEN TAGLIATELLE WITH TOMATO SAUCE

Tagliatelle Verdi con Salsa Burro e Oro

Follow this surprisingly delicate dish with any roast meat or poultry.

MAKES 4 SERVINGS

Basic Spinach Pasta Dough, page 41,
   made with 2 cups all-purpose flour
1½ cups Plain Tomato Sauce, page 208
¼ cup butter

½ cup whipping cream
Salt and freshly ground pepper to taste
⅓ cup freshly grated Parmesan cheese
   plus additional for serving

Prepare noodles, page 41, from Basic Spinach Pasta Dough. Prepare Plain Tomato Sauce.

Melt butter in a medium saucepan. When butter foams, add tomato sauce and cream. Season with salt and pepper. Simmer uncovered 8 to 10 minutes. Fill a very large saucepan two-thirds full with salted water. Bring water to a boil. Add noodles. Bring water back to a boil and cook noodles uncovered until tender but firm to the bite.

Drain noodles and place in a warm deep dish or bowl. Add sauce and toss gently until mixed. Add ⅓ cup Parmesan cheese and toss to blend. Serve immediately with additional Parmesan cheese.

ᗧ

GREEN AND YELLOW TAGLIATELLE WITH MUSHROOM SAUCE

Tagliatelle Verdi e Gialle con Salsa di Funghi

I cooked this beautiful dish for a dinner party and I received applause. What a reward!

MAKES 8 SERVINGS

Basic Spinach Pasta Dough, page 41 made with 2 cups all-purpose flour	**1 cup whipping cream**
Basic Egg Pasta Dough, page 40, made with 2¼ cups all-purpose flour	**2 tablespoons chopped parsley**
1 pound small white mushrooms	**Salt and freshly ground pepper to taste**
¼ cup butter	**⅓ cup freshly grated Parmesan cheese plus additional for serving**

Prepare noodles from Basic Spinach Pasta Dough and Basic Egg Pasta Dough

Wash and dry mushrooms thoroughly and slice thin. Melt butter in a large skillet. When butter foams, add mushrooms. Sauté over high heat until lightly colored. Stir in cream, parsley and salt and pepper. Simmer 2 to 3 minutes or until cream begins to thicken.

Fill a very large saucepan two-thirds full with salted water. Bring water to a boil. Add noodles. Bring water back to a boil and cook noodles uncovered until tender but firm to the bite.

Drain noodles and place in skillet with sauce; add ⅓ cup Parmesan cheese. Toss noodles, sauce and cheese over medium heat until sauce coats noodles, 20 to 30 seconds. Serve immediately with additional Parmesan cheese.

PAPPARDELLE BAKED WITH
SMOKED MOZZARELLA AND FRESH TOMATOES

Pappardelle Pasticciate con Mozzarella Affumicata

These wide, baked noodles are laced by melted, creamy mozzarella, butter and diced tomatoes—a most beautiful sight.

MAKES 4 SERVINGS

Basic Egg Pasta Dough, page 40, made
    with 2¼ cups all-purpose flour
6 tablespoons butter
4 medium, ripe tomatoes, diced
2 ounces smoked mozzarella, diced

2 ounces whole-milk mozzarella, diced
10 to 12 fresh basil leaves, shredded
Salt to taste
¼ cup freshly grated Parmesan cheese

Prepare pasta dough and roll out into pasta sheets. Let the pasta sheets dry about 5 minutes, then with a scalloped pastry wheel, cut them into broad noodles, 2 inches wide and 6 inches long.

Preheat oven to 400F (205C). Butter a 13 × 9-inch baking dish. Fill a very large saucepan two-thirds full with salted water. Bring water to a boil. Add the noodles. Bring water back to a boil and cook noodles uncovered until tender but firm to the bite, 7 to 8 minutes.

While the noodles are cooking, melt the butter in a large skillet over medium heat. When the butter foams, add the diced tomatoes. Cook 1 to 2 minutes, stirring. Drain the noodles and add to the tomatoes. Add mozzarella and basil, season lightly with salt and mix well. Put everything into the baking dish and sprinkle with Parmesan cheese. Bake 4 to 5 minutes or until the cheese is melted. Divide the pasta into 4 portions and serve immediately.

Note
After baking, the pasta will be "tied" together with the cheeses. To serve it, divide the pasta into servings with a knife.

PAPPARDELLE WITH MUSHROOM SAUCE

Pappardelle con i Funghi

Pappardelle are the widest of all noodles.

❀ MAKES 6 SERVINGS

Basic Egg Pasta Dough, page 40, made
   with 3 cups all-purpose flour
1½ pounds small white mushrooms
5 tablespoons olive oil
2 garlic cloves, finely chopped

¾ cup dry white wine
3 tablespoons chopped parsley
Salt and freshly ground pepper to taste
2 tablespoons butter

Prepare Basic Egg Pasta Dough. Dry pasta sheets 10 minutes. With a fluted pastry wheel, cut each sheet of pasta into broad strips ½ inch wide to make pappardelle. Arrange noodles in soft piles on a large tablecloth.

Wash and dry mushrooms thoroughly and slice thin. Heat oil in a large skillet. Add garlic and sauté over medium heat about 1 minute. When garlic begins to color, add sliced mushrooms. Sauté mushrooms over high heat until lightly colored. Add wine. Cook until wine is reduced by half, stirring constantly. Add parsley and cook 1 minute longer. Season with salt and pepper.

Fill a very large saucepan two-thirds full with salted water. Bring water to a boil. Add noodles. Bring water back to a boil and cook noodles uncovered until tender but firm to the bite.

Drain noodles and place in skillet with sauce; add butter. Toss noodles, sauce and butter over medium heat until sauce coats noodles, 20 to 30 seconds. Serve immediately.

BAKED MACARONI

Maccheroni al Forno

Try to resist a second helping!

§❧ **MAKES 4 SERVINGS**

2 cups Chicken Broth, page 23 or canned
    chicken broth
¼ cup plus 2 tablespoons butter
1 medium onion, finely chopped
1 carrot, finely chopped
4 slices (¼ pound) pancetta, page 4,
    diced

¼ cup tomato paste
Salt and freshly ground pepper to taste
1 pound large, grooved macaroni
Basic White Sauce, page 205, made with
    2 cups milk
½ cup freshly grated Parmesan cheese

Prepare Chicken Broth. Preheat oven to 375F (190C). Butter a 13 × 9-inch baking dish. Melt ¼ cup butter in a medium saucepan. When butter foams, add onion and carrot. Sauté over medium heat until onion is pale yellow. Add pancetta. Sauté until lightly colored. Combine tomato paste and broth and add to saucepan. Simmer uncovered 20 to 25 minutes. Season with salt and pepper.

Fill a very large saucepan two-thirds full with salted water. Bring water to a boil. Add macaroni. Bring water back to a boil and cook macaroni uncovered until tender but firm to the bite, 6 to 8 minutes.

Drain macaroni and place in buttered baking dish. Prepare Basic White Sauce. Stir tomato sauce and white sauce into macaroni; mix to blend. Add ⅓ cup Parmesan cheese; mix gently. Sprinkle remaining Parmesan cheese over macaroni and dot with 2 tablespoons butter. Bake 10 to 15 minutes or until cheese is melted and top is golden. Serve hot.

MACARONI WITH VODKA SAUCE

Maccheroni con la Vodka

This simple sauce is a creation of the Dante restaurant in Bologna.

§◦ MAKES 4 TO 6 SERVINGS

1½ cups **Plain Tomato Sauce, page 208**

¼ cup butter

4 slices (¼ pound) pancetta, page 4,
   diced

⅓ cup vodka

½ cup whipping cream

Salt and freshly ground pepper to taste

1 pound grooved macaroni, such as
   penne or rigatoni

½ cup freshly grated Parmesan cheese

Prepare Plain Tomato Sauce. Melt butter in a large skillet. When butter foams, add pancetta. Sauté over medium heat until lightly colored. Add vodka and stir until it has evaporated. Stir in tomato sauce and cream. Simmer uncovered 8 to 10 minutes. Season with salt and pepper.

Fill a very large saucepan two-thirds full with salted water. Bring water to a boil. Add macaroni. Bring water back to a boil and cook macaroni uncovered until tender but firm to the bite, 8 to 10 minutes.

Drain macaroni and place in skillet with sauce. Toss macaroni and sauce over medium heat until sauce coats macaroni, 20 to 30 seconds. Serve immediately with Parmesan cheese.

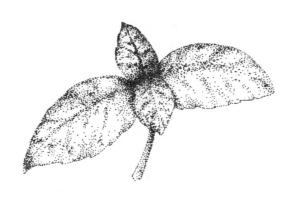

MACARONI WITH HAM AND ASPARAGUS

Maccheroni con Prosciutto Cotto e Asparagi

It takes longer to prepare a frozen dinner than to cook this absolutely delectable dish.

MAKES 4 TO 6 SERVINGS

1½ pounds small asparagus

¼ cup butter

2 medium onions, thinly sliced

½ pound boiled ham, diced

1 cup whipping cream

Salt and freshly ground pepper to taste

1 pound medium-size macaroni, such as penne

⅓ cup freshly grated Parmesan cheese plus additional for serving

Wash asparagus and cut tips off stalks. Reserve stalks for another use. Fill a medium saucepan half full with salted water. Bring water to a boil. Add asparagus tips. Boil about 1 minute or until tender but firm. Drain asparagus.

Melt butter in a large skillet. When butter foams, add onions. Sauté over medium heat until pale yellow. Add drained asparagus and ham. Sauté 1 to 2 minutes. Stir in cream. Simmer 2 minutes or until cream begins to thicken. Season with salt and pepper.

Fill a very large saucepan two-thirds full with salted water. Bring water to a boil. Add macaroni. Bring water back to a boil and cook macaroni uncovered until tender but firm to the bite, 8 to 10 minutes.

Drain macaroni and place in skillet with sauce. Add ⅓ cup Parmesan cheese. Toss macaroni and sauce over medium heat until sauce coats macaroni, 20 to 30 seconds. Serve immediately with additional Parmesan cheese.

TAGLIOLINI WITH SCALLOPS, CREAM AND SAFFRON

Tagliolini con Cape Sante allo Zafferano

If sauce reduces too much, instead of adding more cream add a bit of pasta cooking water.

MAKES 4 SERVINGS

Basic Egg Pasta Dough, page 40, made with 2¼ cups all-purpose flour	**2 garlic cloves, finely minced**
2 tablespoons butter	**1 cup dry white wine**
2 tablespoons olive oil	**2 cups whipping cream**
1 pound scallops, the smallest you can get	**Pinch of powdered saffron**
	Salt to taste
	2 tablespoons chopped parsley

Prepare pasta dough and roll out into pasta sheets. Dry pasta sheets 10 to 15 minutes. Feed pasta sheets through the narrow cutting blades of the pasta machine to make tagliolini. Arrange noodles in soft piles on a large tablecloth.

Melt butter with the oil in a large skillet. When butter foams, add scallops. Sauté over medium heat until scallops are lightly golden, about 1 minute. With a slotted spoon transfer scallops to a plate. Add garlic to the skillet and stir once or twice. Add wine and cook until the wine is almost all reduced. Add cream and saffron. Cook, over medium heat, 4 to 5 minutes. Season lightly with salt. Return scallops to the skillet and cook 1 to 2 minutes longer. Stir in parsley.

Meanwhile fill a large saucepan two-thirds full with salted water. Bring water to a boil and add the noodles. Bring water back to a boil and cook noodles uncovered until tender but firm to the bite, 4 to 6 minutes depending on the freshness of the noodles. Drain noodles and place in skillet with the sauce. Toss noodles with the sauce over medium heat and serve at once.

STRICHETTI WITH GARLIC AND TOMATO SAUCE

Strichetti all'Aglio e Pomodoro

When I first learned to make pasta, this was my favorite one to make and eat.

ℬ **MAKES 6 SERVINGS**

Basic Egg Pasta Dough, page 40, made
    with 3 cups all-purpose flour
2 cups Tomato Sauce Bologna Style, page
    203
⅓ cup olive oil

6 garlic cloves, finely chopped
2 tablespoons chopped parsley
Salt and freshly ground pepper to taste
½ cup freshly grated Parmesan cheese

Prepare Basic Egg Pasta Dough. Cut a small piece of dough and work through the pasta machine until you have a thin sheet of pasta. Cut pasta sheet into rectangles 2 inches wide and 2½ inches long. Pinch the 2 long sides of each rectangle together in the center making butterfly shapes or strichetti. Repeat with remaining dough, rolling out and shaping 1 sheet of pasta at a time. Spread strichetti in a single layer on a large tablecloth to dry.

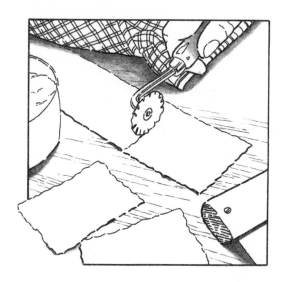

Prepare Tomato Sauce Bologna Style. Heat oil in a medium saucepan. Add garlic and parsley. Sauté 1 minute over medium heat. Just before garlic changes color, add tomato sauce and salt and pepper. Cook uncovered 5 to 8 minutes.

Fill a very large saucepan two-thirds full with salted water. Bring water to a boil. Add strichetti. Bring water back to a boil and cook strichetti uncovered until tender but firm to the bite. Drain strichetti and place in a warm deep dish or bowl. Add sauce. Toss strichetti and sauce gently until mixed. Serve immediately with Parmesan cheese.

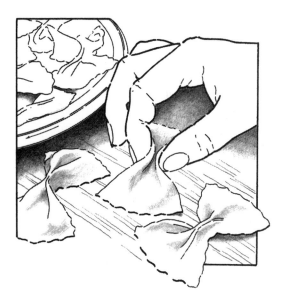

RIGATONI WITH PEPERONATA

Rigatoni con la Peperonata

Peperonata is too good to use only as a side dish so here it is transformed into a superb pasta dish.

§ৡ **MAKES 4 TO 6 SERVINGS**

2 cups Peperonata, page 171
1 pound rigatoni or any large, grooved macaroni
Freshly ground pepper to taste

Prepare Peperonata and keep warm.

Fill a very large saucepan two-thirds full with salted water. Bring water to a boil. Add rigatoni. Bring water back to a boil and cook rigatoni uncovered until tender but firm to the bite, 8 to 10 minutes.

Drain rigatoni and place in a warm deep dish or bowl. Pour Peperonata over rigatoni. Season with pepper. Serve immediately.

ᘄ

FETTUCCINE WITH BUTTER AND CREAM

Fettuccine all'Alfredo

Fettuccine is the Roman name for noodles.

§ৡ **MAKES 4 TO 6 SERVINGS**

Basic Egg Pasta Dough, page 40, made
   with 2¼ cups all-purpose flour
¼ cup butter
1 cup whipping cream

Salt and white pepper to taste
¼ cup freshly grated Parmesan cheese
   plus additional for serving

Prepare noodles from Basic Egg Pasta Dough. Melt butter in a large skillet. When butter foams, add cream. Simmer over medium heat about 2 minutes until slightly thickened. Season with salt and white pepper.

Fill a very large saucepan two-thirds full with salted water. Bring water to a boil. Add noodles. Bring water back to a boil and cook noodles uncovered until tender but firm to the bite.

Drain noodles and place in skillet with cream. Add ¼ cup Parmesan cheese. Toss noodles and sauce over medium heat until sauce coats noodles, 20 to 30 seconds. Serve immediately with additional Parmesan cheese.

༂

SHELLS WITH SAUSAGE AND TOMATO RAGÙ

Conchiglie con Ragù di Salsiccia e Pomodoro

This appetizing sauce, from Emilia-Romagna, can be served over any kind of pasta.

MAKES 4 SERVINGS

2 tablespoons unsalted butter

2 tablespoons olive oil

1 large leek, white part only, rinsed and finely minced

1 large carrot, finely minced

1 garlic clove, finely chopped

½ pound mild Italian sausage

¼ pound sliced pancetta, page 4, diced

1 cup full-bodied red wine

4 cups canned imported Italian tomatoes with juice, put through a strainer or a food mill to remove seeds

1 cup Chicken Broth, page 23, or canned chicken broth

Salt to taste

2 tablespoons chopped parsley

1 pound pasta shells or penne

⅓ cup freshly grated Parmesan cheese

Melt butter with oil in a medium saucepan. Add leek and carrot. Cook over medium heat, stirring, until the vegetables are lightly golden and soft. Add the garlic and stir once or twice. Remove the casing from the sausage and finely chop meat. Increase heat and add sausage and pancetta to the saucepan. Cook, stirring, until the sausage and pancetta are lightly colored. Add the wine. Cook until the wine is almost all reduced. Add the tomatoes and broth. Season with salt. Reduce heat and simmer uncovered 15 to 20 minutes, then stir in parsley.

Fill a very large saucepan two-thirds full with salted water. Bring water to a boil. Add the shells. Bring water back to a boil and cook shells uncovered 7 to 10 minutes until tender but firm to the bite. Drain shells and place in a warm deep dish or bowl. Add sauce and toss gently. Serve immediately with a generous sprinkling of grated Parmesan cheese.

BAKED CANNELLONI

Cannelloni al Forno

An elegant dish for a party, it can be prepared ahead.

MAKES ABOUT 20 CANNELLONI, 6 TO 8 SERVINGS

2 cups Plain Tomato Sauce, page 208

Basic White Sauce, page 205, made with
   3 cups milk

Meat Filling

3 tablespoons butter

1 pound chicken breasts, boned, skinned,
   chopped into small pieces

¼ pound prosciutto, page 4, diced

¼ pound mortadella, diced

½ cup freshly grated Parmesan cheese

½ teaspoon freshly grated nutmeg

2 or 3 tablespoons whipping cream, if
   needed

Salt and freshly ground pepper to taste

Basic Egg Pasta Dough, page 40, made
   with 4½ cups all-purpose flour

½ cup freshly grated Parmesan cheese

3 tablespoons butter

Prepare Plain Tomato Sauce. Prepare Basic White Sauce.

Prepare Meat Filling: Melt butter in a medium skillet. When butter foams, add chicken pieces. Sauté over medium heat until lightly colored. Put chicken and all other ingredients except cream in a blender or food processor. Blend to a paste. If mixture is too dry, add cream. Season with salt and pepper. Prepare Basic Egg Pasta Dough. Dry pasta sheets 10 minutes. Cut sheets into 5-inch squares.

Preheat oven to 400F (205C). Butter a 13 × 9-inch baking dish. Fill a very large saucepan two-thirds full with salted water. Bring water to a boil. Add 7 or 8 pasta squares. Bring water back to a boil and cook pasta uncovered 10 seconds. With a large slotted spoon, place pasta in a large bowl of cold water. Remove pasta squares immediately and lay on kitchen towels. Pat dry with another towel. Repeat with remaining pasta squares.

Place 1 or 2 tablespoons Meat Filling down center of each dried pasta square. Fold 2 opposite edges of pasta over filling to make a tube. Place cannelloni with folded edges down, close together in a single layer in buttered baking dish. Spoon tomato sauce over cannelloni. Cover with white sauce. Sprinkle with Parmesan cheese and dot with butter. Bake 10 to 15 minutes or until cheese is melted and cannelloni are lightly golden. Let stand 5 to 10 minutes before serving.

SPAGHETTI WITH SPRING VEGETABLES

Spaghetti Primavera

This dish captures the bountifulness of spring.

℘ MAKES 4 TO 6 SERVINGS

5 medium tomatoes	1 medium onion, thinly sliced
¼ pound small asparagus	Salt and freshly ground pepper to taste
1 medium zucchini	3 tablespoons chopped parsley
¼ pound small white mushrooms	2 garlic cloves, finely chopped
1 large red or green sweet pepper	1 pound spaghetti
5 tablespoons olive oil	

Peel, seed and dice tomatoes. Wash asparagus and cut tips off stalks. Reserve stalks for another use. Wash and dry zucchini and mushrooms thoroughly; cut into thin slices. Wash pepper and cut into short thin strips.

Heat oil in large skillet. Add pepper strips and sauté over medium heat 5 to 6 minutes. Add onion, zucchini, asparagus tips and mushrooms. Sauté 4 to 5 minutes. Add diced tomatoes and salt and pepper. Cook uncovered over medium heat 10 minutes, stirring frequently. Stir in parsley and garlic. Taste and adjust for seasoning.

Fill a very large saucepan two-thirds full with salted water. Bring water to a boil. Add spaghetti. Bring water back to a boil and cook spaghetti uncovered until tender but firm to the bite, 8 to 10 minutes. Drain spaghetti and place in a warm deep dish or bowl. Pour sauce over spaghetti. Serve immediately.

SPAGHETTI WITH TUNA SAUCE

Spaghetti con il Tonno

Do not serve cheese over this pasta; be generous with the pepper instead.

MAKES 4 SERVINGS

¼ cup olive oil

4 flat anchovy fillets, finely chopped

2 garlic cloves, finely chopped

1 (28-ounce) can crushed Italian-style or
    whole tomatoes

Salt and freshly ground pepper to taste

1 (7-ounce) can tuna in olive oil, drained,
    flaked

3 tablespoons chopped parsley

1 pound spaghetti

Heat oil in a medium saucepan. Add anchovies and garlic. Sauté gently about 1 minute; do not let garlic turn brown. Press tomatoes through a food mill or sieve to remove seeds (page 208). Stir tomato pulp into saucepan. Simmer uncovered 25 to 30 minutes or until sauce reduces to a medium-thick consistency. Season with salt and pepper. Stir in tuna and parsley. Simmer 5 minutes.

Fill a very large saucepan two-thirds full with salted water. Bring water to a boil. Add spaghetti. Bring water back to a boil and cook spaghetti uncovered until tender but firm to the bite, 8 to 10 minutes.

Drain spaghetti and place in a warm deep dish or bowl. Add sauce and toss gently until mixed. Serve immediately.

GREEN LASAGNE BOLOGNA STYLE

Lasagne Verdi alla Bolognese

In this celebrated dish, each ingredient complements the other without losing its individuality.

MAKES 8 SERVINGS

4 to 4½ cups Bolognese Meat Sauce, page 206

Basic White Sauce, page 205, made with 5 cups milk

Basic Spinach Pasta Dough, page 41, made with 3 cups all-purpose flour

2 cups freshly grated Parmesan cheese

3 tablespoons butter

Prepare Bolognese Meat Sauce. Prepare Basic White Sauce. Prepare Basic Spinach Pasta Dough and cut into lengths to fit a 13 × 9-inch baking dish. Dry pasta sheets 10 minutes.

Preheat oven to 400F (205C). Butter baking dish. Fill a very large saucepan two-thirds full with salted water. Bring water to a boil. Add 4 pasta sheets. Bring water back to a boil and cook pasta uncovered 10 seconds. With a large slotted spoon, place pasta in a large bowl of cold water. Remove pasta sheets immediately and lay on kitchen towels. Pat dry with another towel. Repeat with remaining pasta sheets.

Cover bottom of buttered baking dish with a layer of dried pasta sheets. Spread some meat sauce over pasta. Follow with a layer of Basic White Sauce, about ½ cup. Sprinkle with about ⅓ cup Parmesan cheese. Repeat with five more layers, ending with Parmesan cheese. Dot with butter.

Bake 15 to 20 minutes or until top of lasagne is golden. Let stand 5 to 10 minutes before serving.

TORTELLINI WITH CREAM SAUCE

Tortellini alla Panna

Tortellini are instantly recognized as the best contribution of Bolognese cuisine to Italian gastronomy.

MAKES 5 TO 6 SERVINGS

Meat Filling
2 tablespoons butter
1 pound pork loin, finely chopped
½ cup dry white wine
2 eggs
½ teaspoon freshly grated nutmeg
¼ pound mortadella
¼ pound prosciutto, page 4
¾ cup freshly grated Parmesan cheese
2 to 3 tablespoons whipping cream, if needed
Salt and freshly ground pepper to taste

Basic Egg Pasta Dough, page 40 made with 3 cups all-purpose flour

Cream Sauce
¼ cup butter
1 cup whipping cream
1 teaspoon salt

⅓ cup freshly grated Parmesan cheese plus additional for serving

Prepare Meat Filling: Melt butter in a small skillet. When butter foams, add pork. Sauté over medium heat until light golden. Add wine. Reduce heat and cook covered 10 to 12 minutes. Put pork mixture and all other ingredients except cream in a blender or food processor. Blend to a paste. If mixture is too dry, add cream. Season with salt and pepper. Refrigerate.

Prepare Basic Egg Pasta Dough. Cut a small piece of dough and work through the pasta machine until you have a very thin sheet of pasta. Cut pasta into 2-inch circles using a small glass or cookie cutter. Put ½ teaspoon filling in the center of each circle. Fold circles in half and press firmly to seal edges to make tortellini. Bend each tortellini around your finger, pressing 1 pointed end over the other. Repeat with remaining dough, rolling out and filling 1 sheet of pasta at a time. Dust 2 or 3 large plates or trays with flour. Place tortellini on plates or trays. Turn tortellini over every couple of hours, until completely dry. Refrigerate uncovered until ready to use.

Prepare Cream Sauce: Melt butter in a large skillet. When butter foams, add cream. Simmer 2 or 3 minutes until slightly thickened. Add salt.

Fill a very large saucepan two-thirds full with salted water. Bring water to a boil. Add tortellini. Bring water back to a boil and cook tortellini uncovered until tender but firm to the bite. Drain tortellini and place in skillet with sauce. Add ⅓ cup Parmesan cheese. Toss tortellini and sauce over low heat until sauce coats tortellini, 20 to 30 seconds. Serve immediately with additional Parmesan cheese.

TORTELLINI WITH BOLOGNESE MEAT SAUCE

Tortellini col Ragù

With a few advance preparations, you can relax and enjoy your company.

MAKES 5 TO 6 SERVINGS

Tortellini, page 66
1½ to 2 cups Bolognese Meat Sauce, page 206
½ cup freshly grated Parmesan cheese

Prepare and fill tortellini. Prepare Bolognese Meat Sauce and keep warm.

Fill a very large saucepan two-thirds full with salted water. Bring water to a boil. Add tortellini. Bring water back to a boil and cook tortellini uncovered until tender but firm to the bite.

Drain tortellini and place in a warm deep dish or bowl. Add meat sauce and toss gently until mixed. Serve immediately with Parmesan cheese.

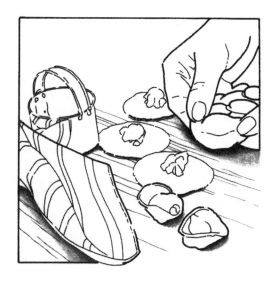

TORTELLONI WITH RICOTTA CHEESE AND PARSLEY

Tortelloni di Ricotta e Prezzemolo

Tortelloni are traditionally served in Bologna on the night before Christmas.

⅓ MAKES 6 SERVINGS

Cheese Filling
1 egg yolk
1 pound ricotta cheese
⅓ cup chopped parsley
½ cup freshly grated Parmesan cheese
½ teaspoon freshly grated nutmeg
Salt to taste

Tomato-Cream Sauce
2 tablespoons butter

1½ cups Plain Tomato Sauce, page 208
½ cup whipping cream
Salt and freshly ground pepper to taste

Basic Egg Pasta Dough, page 40, made
   with 3 cups all-purpose flour
2 tablespoons butter
⅓ cup freshly grated Parmesan cheese
   plus additional for serving

Prepare Cheese Filling: Beat egg yolk in a large bowl. Add ricotta cheese, parsley, Parmesan cheese and nutmeg; mix to blend. Season with salt. Refrigerate until needed.

Prepare Tomato-Cream Sauce: Melt butter in a medium saucepan. Add Plain Tomato Sauce and cream. Season with salt and pepper. Simmer 5 to 10 minutes. Let stand at room temperature.

Prepare Basic Egg Pasta Dough. Cut a small piece of dough and work through the pasta machine until you have a very thin sheet of pasta. Cut pasta into 3-inch circles using a glass or a cookie cutter. Put 1 teaspoon filling in the center of each circle. Fold circles in half and press firmly to seal edges to make tortelloni. Bend each tortelloni around your finger, pressing 1 pointed end over the other. Repeat with remaining dough, rolling out and filling 1 sheet of pasta at a time. Dust 2 or 3 large plates or trays with flour. Place tortelloni on plates or trays. Turn tortelloni over every couple of hours until completely dry. Refrigerate uncovered until ready to use.

Fill a very large saucepan two-thirds full with salted water. Bring water to a boil. Add tortelloni. Bring water back to a boil and cook tortelloni uncovered until tender but firm to the bite, page 38. Drain tortelloni and place in a warm deep dish or bowl. Add butter, Tomato-Cream Sauce and ⅓ cup Parmesan cheese. Toss gently until mixed. Serve immediately with additional Parmesan cheese.

Variation

Make green tortelloni using Basic Spinach Pasta Dough, page 41, made with 3 cups all-purpose flour.

LINGUINE WITH RED CLAM SAUCE

Linguine con le Vongole

Linguine belong to the same family as spaghetti but they are flat.

MAKES 4 TO 6 SERVINGS

1 cup Plain Tomato Sauce, page 208	2 tablespoons chopped parsley
4 pounds small fresh clams	3 flat anchovy fillets, finely chopped
5 tablespoons olive oil	Salt and freshly ground pepper to taste
1 cup water	1 pound linguine
3 garlic cloves, finely chopped	

Prepare Plain Tomato Sauce.

Soak clams in cold water 15 minutes. Scrub clams with a brush and rinse thoroughly. Put clams, 2 tablespoons of the oil and 1 cup water in a large saucepan; cover pan. Cook over high heat until clams open, 1 to 2 minutes. Remove clam meat from shells. Strain pan juices and place in a small saucepan. Bring to a boil and cook uncovered until liquid is reduced to about ½ cup. Set aside.

Heat 3 tablespoons oil in a medium saucepan. Add garlic, parsley and anchovies. Sauté over medium heat about 1 minute. When garlic changes color, add tomato sauce, reserved clam juice and season with salt and pepper. Cook 5 minutes. Add clam meat and cook 1 to 2 minutes longer.

Fill a very large saucepan two-thirds full with salted water. Bring water to a boil. Add linguine. Bring water back to a boil and cook linguine uncovered until tender but firm to the bite, 8 to 10 minutes.

Drain linguine and place in a warm deep dish or bowl. Add sauce and toss gently until mixed. Serve immediately.

AGNOLOTTI GENOA STYLE

Agnolotti alla Genovese

In many regions, agnolotti and ravioli are the same shape but their fillings are different.

MAKES 6 SERVINGS

Meat Filling

½ cup Chicken Broth, page 23, or
  canned chicken broth

1 (10-ounce) pkg. frozen spinach, thawed

3 tablespoons butter

2 large onions, thinly sliced

1 pound pork loin, cut in 1-inch cubes

¾ cup dry white wine

1 tablespoon chopped parsley

2 tablespoons chopped fresh basil or
  parsley

2 eggs

½ teaspoon dried chervil

Salt and freshly ground pepper to taste

¾ cup freshly grated Parmesan cheese

Basic Egg Pasta Dough, page 40, made
  with 3 cups all-purpose flour

¼ cup butter, at room temperature

½ cup freshly grated Parmesan cheese
  plus additional for serving

Prepare Meat Filling: Prepare Chicken Broth. Squeeze spinach to remove as much moisture as possible. Melt butter in a medium skillet. When butter foams, add onions and pork. Sauté 3 to 4 minutes over medium heat until light golden. Stir in wine. Cook until wine has evaporated. Add broth. Cook uncovered 15 minutes or until all moisture has evaporated. Stir occasionally. Add spinach, parsley and basil or extra parsley. Cook 1 to 2 minutes longer. Put pork mixture in a blender or food processor. Add eggs and chervil and blend to a paste. Season with salt and pepper. Place mixture in a bowl. Add Parmesan cheese and mix thoroughly. Refrigerate.

Prepare Basic Egg Pasta Dough. Cut small pieces of dough and work through the pasta machine until you have thin sheets of pasta. Cut pasta sheets into strips 4 inches wide. Place 1 teaspoon filling every 2 inches down the center of each strip of pasta. Fold sheets in half over filling. Press edges together to seal. With a pastry cutter, cut pasta strips into squares, cutting between filling to make agnolotti. Dust 2 or 3 large plates or trays with flour. Place agnolotti on plates or trays. Turn agnolotti over every 2 to 3 hours until completely dry. Refrigerate uncovered until ready to use.

Fill a very large saucepan two-thirds full with salted water. Bring water to a boil. Add agnolotti. Bring water back to a boil and cook agnolotti uncovered until tender but firm to the bite. Drain agnolotti and place in a warm deep dish or bowl. Add butter and ½ cup Parmesan cheese. Toss gently until mixed. Serve immediately with additional Parmesan cheese.

TRENETTE WITH PESTO SAUCE

Trenette col Pesto

If you lived in the Liguria region of Italy you would call noodles trenette.

§ᴥ **MAKES 6 SERVINGS**

Basic Egg Pasta Dough, page 40 made with 3 cups all-purpose flour
½ to ¾ cup Pesto Sauce, page 205

Prepare noodles from Basic Egg Pasta Dough. Prepare Pesto Sauce and let stand at room temperature.

Fill a very large saucepan two-thirds full with salted water. Bring water to a boil. Add noodles. Bring water back to a boil and cook noodles uncovered until tender but firm to the bite.

Drain noodles and place in a warm deep dish or bowl. Add Pesto Sauce and toss gently until mixed. Serve immediately.

Gnocchi, Polenta and Risotto

Gnocchi is the general name for Italian dumplings. There are many kinds including potato, spinach and spinach with cheese. This light Italian version of dumplings is a melt-in-your mouth delicacy. Gnocchi are served as a first course with an incredible array of sauces. In a way, gnocchi and pasta are very much alike. They could be eaten with a different sauce every day for weeks without a dish being repeated. When you serve gnocchi, follow the same guidelines as for serving pasta. Gnocchi are only the first course so serve moderate portions with a small amount of sauce.

With practice, you will find gnocchi are really simple to make. Have fun experimenting with the recipes in this chapter. Then go on to dazzle family and friends with superb dishes.

Polenta

Polenta is made from cornmeal and probably dates back further than any dish in Italian cuisine. It was a staple of life in Roman times when it was called *pulmentum* or puls. At that time, polenta was probably made of barley and later of wheat. When corn was brought to Europe from North America, polenta became the dish it is today.

In most Northern Italian kitchens, polenta is more than a food, it is a rite. It was made originally in a large copper kettle called a *paiolo*. The kettle was suspended from a thick chain directly over a burning fire. No country kitchen, no matter how poor, was without a fireplace.

In the cities, polenta was made on a charcoal- or wood-burning stove. While the woman of the house stirred the cornmeal mixture, the family gathered around, talking and sipping wine.

I remember as a very young girl during wartime, sometimes, somehow, my family would get cornmeal. Then all of us gathered around the stove to watch my mother engage in the ritual of polenta making. She would reach inside the copper kettle and stir the mixture constantly with a long-handled wooden spoon. And when the golden polenta was poured onto a large, wooden board, it resembled a steaming yellow moon.

Polenta is almost never served by itself. It usually accompanies meat, poultry, fish, cheese or rich sauces. Polenta can be fried, baked, broiled or eaten simply with butter and cheese. When you make polenta, be sure to cook it over medium heat and stir it with a long-handled wooden spoon. The long handle is necessary because polenta will bubble and spit while it thickens. This may leave you with some unwanted tiny burns if you are stirring directly over the kettle.

Polenta is a satisfying food, perfect for cold winter nights, for informal dinners, robust appetites and good company.

Risotto

When I started teaching in California a few years ago, I was amazed at the number of people who had never tasted or heard of *risotto*. Risotto is an important part of Northern Italian cuisine and in many regions is more popular than pasta.

Risotto is produced by cooking rice in a particular way, with a technique that is uniquely Northern Italian. Italy is the greatest producer of rice in Europe. It is also one of the largest consumers. There are many kinds of risotto, made with the same technique but with different ingredients. Risotto can be made with herbs, vegetables, cheese, sausages, shellfish and many other ingredients. But what is a risotto exactly?

A risotto is rice that is first sautéed briefly with chopped onions in butter. Then enough hot chicken broth is added to cover the rice. The rice is cooked and stirred until the broth is absorbed. Then more broth is added. It is important to stir constantly or the rice will stick. This technique will produce a delicious, creamy risotto with each grain of rice tender yet firm to the bite.

Italian rice, which is thick and short-grained, is perfect for risotto. The best-known exported Italian rice is *arborio*. It is available in Italian groceries and gourmet shops. Short-grain California pearl rice can be used in place of Italian rice. It is similar to the rice used in Italy. Do not select short-grain rice coated with glucose and talc. It is sticky when cooked and is processed for the Asian market. Do not wash short-grain California pearl rice or any rice that you use for risotto.

Risotto should be made at the last moment or it will dry out, and reheating makes it become soft and mushy. If you have all the ingredients arranged on a tray and the broth is piping hot, it will be very simple to cook a risotto. A risotto is always served as a first course and is only rarely served with meat. One meat dish it is served with is Veal Shanks Milan Style, page 151.

In the summer of 1980, my husband and I took a gastronomical tour through Northern Italy. Wherever we went, risotto appeared on menus as often as pasta, in incredibly varied and mouthwatering concoctions.

After you have cooked several risottos, I know you will feel as I do, completely hooked on this marvelous Northern Italian dish.

BASIC POTATO DUMPLINGS

Gnocchi di Patate

Transform the humble potato into a melt-in-your-mouth dumpling.

§ **MAKES 8 SERVINGS**

8 medium potatoes, preferably russets

1 egg yolk

1 tablespoon salt

2 to 2½ cups all-purpose flour

1 tablespoon vegetable oil

¼ cup butter

½ cup freshly grated Parmesan cheese

Preheat oven to 350F (175C). With a fork, puncture potatoes in several places. Bake 1 hour or until tender. Remove insides of baked potatoes; discard skins. Mash hot potatoes through a ricer or food mill into a large bowl; let cool slightly.

Add egg yolk, 1 tablespoon salt and 2 cups flour; mix well. Put potato mixture on a working surface or wooden board and knead into a ball. Mixture should be soft and pliable and slightly sticky. If it is too sticky, add more flour. Lightly flour working surface and your hands.

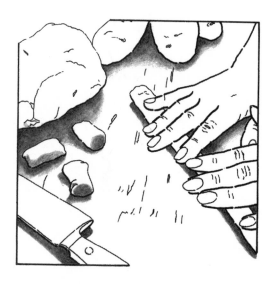

Break dough into pieces the size of large eggs. Shape pieces into rolls about the thickness of your thumb. Cut rolls into 1-inch pieces. Hold a fork with its tines resting on a work surface at a 45° angle and the inside curve toward you. Take a dumpling roll and press it with your index finger against the outside curve of the fork at the tip end. Quickly slide dumpling up and along the length of the tines, pressing with index finger. Remove finger and let dumpling fall back onto work surface. Grooves made by fork and finger indentation will absorb any sauce served with dumplings. Repeat with remaining dumpling rolls. Arrange dumplings on a floured tray or large plate.

Fill a large saucepan two-thirds full with salted water. Bring water to a boil. Add oil and dumplings. When dumplings come to surface of water, cook 10 to 12 seconds. If dumplings remain in water any longer they will absorb water and become too soft. Remove dumplings with a slotted spoon or strainer, draining against side of saucepan. Place in a warm dish. Serve hot with butter and Parmesan cheese or your favorite sauce.

Variation
Potatoes can be boiled instead of baked. Do not puncture potatoes before cooking or they will absorb water, making it necessary to add extra flour to dumpling mixture.

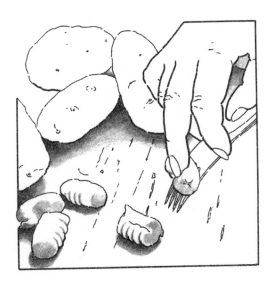

POTATO DUMPLINGS WITH GORGONZOLA SAUCE

Gnocchi di Patate al Gorgonzola

There is no substitute for the distinctive flavor of Gorgonzola.

❧ MAKES 8 SERVINGS

Basic Potato Dumplings, page 78
¼ cup butter
½ cup whipping cream
¼ pound Gorgonzola cheese, crumbled

Salt and freshly ground pepper to taste
1 tablespoon vegetable oil
⅓ cup freshly grated Parmesan cheese

Mix and shape Basic Potato Dumplings.

Melt butter in a large skillet. When butter foams, add cream and bring to a boil. Add Gorgonzola cheese. Stir and cook 3 to 4 minutes over low heat, until cheese is melted and cream begins to thicken. Season with salt and pepper.

Fill a large saucepan two-thirds full with salted water. Bring water to a boil. Add oil and dumplings. When dumplings come to surface of water, cook 10 to 12 seconds.

Remove dumplings with a slotted spoon or strainer, draining against side of saucepan. Place dumplings in sauce. Gently stir in Parmesan cheese. Cook 30 to 40 seconds or until dumplings are coated with sauce. Serve immediately.

POTATO DUMPLINGS WITH PESTO SAUCE

Gnocchi di Patate col Pesto

For perfect dumplings, use starchy potatoes not waxy ones.

🐚 **MAKES 8 SERVINGS**

Basic Potato Dumplings, page 78	**1 tablespoon vegetable oil**
½ cup Pesto Sauce, page 205	**2 tablespoons butter**
10 whole walnuts	**½ cup freshly grated Parmesan cheese**

Mix and shape Basic Potato Dumplings. Prepare Pesto Sauce and let stand at room temperature. Chop walnuts very fine.

Fill a large saucepan two-thirds full with salted water. Bring water to a boil. Add oil and dumplings. When dumplings come to surface of water, cook 10 to 12 seconds.

Remove dumplings with a slotted spoon or strainer, draining against side of saucepan. Place on a warm platter. Add butter, Pesto Sauce and chopped walnuts; mix gently. Serve immediately with Parmesan cheese.

RICOTTA DUMPLINGS WITH
MIXED MUSHROOMS AND PROSCIUTTO SAUCE

Gnocchi di Ricotta ai Funghi Misti e Prosciutto

Mushrooms cooked this way, become even more flavorful—great over gnocchi or pasta.

MAKES 4 TO 6 SERVINGS

1 pound whole-milk ricotta

1½ cups all-purpose unbleached flour

1 teaspoon salt

1 tablespoon butter

1 tablespoon chopped parsley

Mixed Mushrooms and Prosciutto Sauce

⅓ cup olive oil

¾ pound mixed mushrooms, such as

white cultivated mushrooms, brown mushrooms, chanterelles or shiitake, wiped clean and thinly sliced

3 garlic cloves, finely minced

4 anchovy fillets, chopped

¼ pound sliced prosciutto, page 4, cut into small strips

½ cup dry white wine

Salt and freshly ground pepper to taste

In a large bowl, combine ricotta with flour and salt; mix well with your hands to incorporate. Put the mixture on a wooden board and knead gently into a ball. At this point the dough should be smooth, soft and pliable and just a bit sticky. Knead in a little extra flour if dough is too sticky.

Flour the board lightly and break the dough into pieces the size of a small orange. Shape pieces into rolls about the thickness of your thumb. Cut rolls into 1-inch pieces. Hold a fork with its tines resting against a work surface at a 45° angle and the inside curve toward you. Take a little dumpling and press it with your index finger against the outside curve of the fork at the tip end. Quickly slide dumpling up along the length of the tines, pressing with the index finger. Remove finger and let dumpling fall back onto work surface. (Groves made by fork and finger indentation will absorb the sauce.) Repeat with remaining dumplings. Arrange dumplings on a floured tray or large plate. (Dumplings can be prepared several hours or a day ahead of time and refrigerated uncovered.)

Prepare sauce: Heat the oil in a large skillet. Add mushrooms in batches if necessary to avoid crowding the skillet or the mushrooms will "stew" instead of browning. Sauté over high heat, stirring, until they begin to color. Add the garlic, anchovies and prosciutto and stir once or twice. Add the wine. Cook and stir until the wine is almost all reduced. Season with salt and several twists of pepper.

Meanwhile fill a very large saucepan two-thirds full with salted water. Bring water to a boil. Add the gnocchi. When gnocchi come back to the surface of the water cook 20 to 30 seconds.

Remove gnocchi with a slotted spoon or strainer, draining against the side of saucepan. Place gnocchi in skillet with mushrooms. Add the butter and the gnocchi, sprinkle with parsley and mix well. Serve at once.

SWISS CHARD AND RICOTTA GNOCCHI

Gnocchi di Bietola e Ricotta

The leaves of fresh Swiss chard, boiled and chopped very fine, give color and a somewhat sweeter flavor to this classic gnocchi. Traditionally, the favorite "sauce" for these gnocchi, is simply sweet, unsalted butter and freshly grated Parmigiano-Reggiano cheese. Fresh spinach can be used instead of Swiss chard.

MAKES 4 TO 6 SERVINGS

Swiss Chard and Ricotta Gnocchi

1 bunch (about 1 pound)
   Swiss chard

1 large egg

1 pound ricotta

1/2 cup freshly grated Parmigiano-
   Reggiano cheese

2 teaspoons salt

1 1/2 to 1 3/4 cups all-purpose flour

Sauce

3 to 4 tablespoons butter

1/3 to 1/2 cup freshly grated Parmigiano-
   Reggiano cheese

Prepare gnocchi: Remove Swiss chard leaves from stems, and reserve stems for another use. Wash leaves thoroughly in several changes of cold water. Bring a large pot of salted water to a boil, add Swiss chard and cook uncovered until leaves are tender, 3 to 5 minutes. Drain chard and cool. Squeeze leaves with your hands to remove as much water as possible. Place leaves on a cutting board and chop them very fine. (The leaves can also be chopped in a food processor; be careful not to puree them.) Makes approximately 2/3 cup chopped chard.

Break egg in a large bowl and beat it with a fork. Add chard and mix well with egg. Add ricotta, Parmigiano, salt and 1 1/2 cups of flour. Make dough and shape gnocchi as instructed in Basic Ricotta Gnocchi, page 85.

Bring a large pot of boiling water to a boil. Add 1 tablespoon of salt and gnocchi. Cook uncovered over high heat until gnocchi rise to surface of the water, 1 to 2 minutes.

While gnocchi are cooking, make sauce: Melt butter in a large skillet over medium heat. Remove gnocchi with a large slotted spoon or a skimmer, draining off excess water against side of pot, and place in skillet. Season lightly with salt and add about half of the Parmigiano. Stir over medium heat until gnocchi and butter are well combined. Taste, adjust seasoning and serve with remaining Parmigiano.

BASIC RICOTTA GNOCCHI

Gnocchi di Ricotta

❦ MAKES 4 TO 6 SERVINGS

1 pound whole-milk ricotta

⅓ cup freshly grated Parmigiano-
   Reggiano cheese

2 teaspoons salt

1 large egg, lightly beaten in a small
   bowl

1 to 1½ cups all-purpose flour

In a large bowl, combine all ingredients with 1 cup of flour. Mix well with your hands until ricotta and flour are evenly incorporated and mixture sticks together into a rough dough.

Transfer mixture to a wooden board and knead lightly, gradually adding remaining flour if dough sticks heavily to board and to your hands. Knead dough 2 to 3 minutes, dusting it lightly with flour if needed, until dough is smooth, pliable and just a bit sticky.

Cut off a piece of dough, about size of an orange. Flour your hands lightly. (Do not flour working area or dough will not slide smoothly.) Using both hands, roll out piece of dough with a light back-and-forth motion into a roll of about the thickness of your index finger. Cut roll into 1-inch pieces.

Hold a fork with its tines against a work board, curved part of fork facing away from you. Starting from curved outside bottom of fork, press each piece of dough with your index finger firmly upward along length of tines. Let gnocchi fall back onto work surface. Repeat with remaining dough until all gnocchi have been formed.

Line a large tray with a clean kitchen towel and flour towel lightly. Arrange gnocchi on towel without crowding them. They can be cooked immediately or kept in refrigerator for several hours.

Bring a large pot of boiling water to a boil. Add 1 tablespoon of salt and gnocchi. Cook uncovered over high heat until gnocchi rise to surface of the water, 1 to 2 minutes.

BASIC POLENTA

Polenta

An ancient dish that was and still is a staple in the Northern Italian diet.

§ᴏ MAKES 6 TO 8 SERVINGS

9 cups water
1 tablespoon salt
3 cups coarse-grain cornmeal

Bring water to a boil in a large heavy pot. Add salt and reduce heat until water is simmering. Take cornmeal by the handful and add to water very slowly, controlling the flow to a thin stream through your fingers. To avoid lumps, stir quickly with a long-handled wooden spoon while adding cornmeal. If necessary, stop adding cornmeal from time to time and beat mixture vigorously. Cook, stirring constantly, 20 to 30 minutes. Polenta will become very thick while cooking. It is done when it comes away cleanly from sides of pot.

Pour polenta onto a large wooden board or a large platter. Wet your hands and smooth out polenta evenly about 2 inches thick. Let cool 5 to 10 minutes or until polenta solidifies. Cut cooled polenta into slices 1 inch wide and 6 inches long. Place slices in individual dishes. Serve hot, covered with your favorite sauce.

Variation

Fried Polenta (*Polenta Fritta*)

Prepare Basic Polenta and let cool completely. Cut cooled polenta into slices 2 inches wide and 6 inches long. Pour oil about 1 inch deep in a large skillet. Heat oil until a 1-inch cube of bread turns golden almost immediately. Fry polenta slices on both sides until light golden. Drain on paper towels. Serve hot.

BAKED POLENTA WITH BOLOGNESE MEAT SAUCE

Polenta Pasticciata

A satisfying dish for robust appetites on a cold night with good company.

MAKES 6 TO 8 SERVINGS

Basic Polenta, page 86	**5 to 6 tablespoons butter**
3 to 4 cups Bolognese Meat Sauce,	**1 cup freshly grated Parmesan cheese**
page 206	

Prepare Basic Polenta and let cool completely. Prepare Bolognese Meat Sauce.

Preheat oven to 400F (205C). Butter a 13 × 9-inch baking dish. Cut cooled polenta into slices 2 inches wide and 6 inches long. Put a third of the sliced polenta in buttered baking dish. Spoon about 1 cup meat sauce over polenta. Dot with about 2 tablespoons butter and sprinkle with 4 to 5 tablespoons Parmesan cheese. Repeat with two more layers of polenta, meat sauce, butter and Parmesan cheese, making three layers.

Bake 15 to 20 minutes or until cheese is melted. Serve immediately.

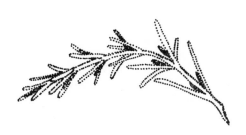

POLENTA WITH SKEWERED MEAT

Polenta con gli Spiedini

In some Italian towns very small birds are used as a delicacy instead of meat in this recipe.

℘ MAKES 6 SERVINGS

½ pound lean veal shoulder

½ pound pork loin

4 or 5 thick slices (½ pound) pancetta, page 4

10 to 12 fresh or dried sage leaves

2 to 3 medium onions, cut into large pieces

Basic Polenta, page 86

¼ cup olive oil

Salt and freshly ground pepper to taste

1½ cups dry white wine

Trim all fat from veal and pork. Cut meat into 1½- to 2-inch cubes. Cut pancetta into cubes. On 6 wooden skewers, alternate veal, pancetta, sage, pork and onions; set aside.

Prepare Basic Polenta. Pour polenta onto a large wooden board or a large platter. Cool 5 minutes. Cut polenta into slices 2 inches wide and 6 inches long.

While polenta cooks, heat oil in a large skillet. Add skewered meat and salt and pepper. Sauté over medium heat 10 minutes, or until meat is lightly browned on all sides. Stir in ¾ cup of the wine. Cook uncovered over medium-low heat 15 to 20 minutes, adding more wine as needed.

Place 2 slices polenta and 1 skewer of meat on each of 6 individual dishes. Spoon some wine sauce from skillet over each serving. Serve immediately.

BAKED POLENTA WITH BUTTER AND PARMESAN CHEESE

Polenta con Burro e Parmigiano al Forno

Polenta can be prepared ahead and refrigerated. Bring to room temperature before baking.

℘ MAKES 6 TO 8 SERVINGS

Basic Polenta, page 86
6 tablespoons butter
1 cup freshly grated Parmesan cheese

Prepare Basic Polenta and let cool completely.

Preheat oven to 375F (190C). Butter a large shallow baking dish. Cut cooled polenta into slices 2 inches wide and 6 inches long. Put slices in buttered baking dish. Dot generously with butter and sprinkle with Parmesan cheese.

Bake 20 minutes or until cheese is melted. For a golden-brown crust, put briefly under preheated broiler. Serve hot.

Variation
Polenta with Fontina Cheese (*Polenta con la Fontina*): Substitute ½ pound sliced Italian fontina cheese for the Parmesan cheese.

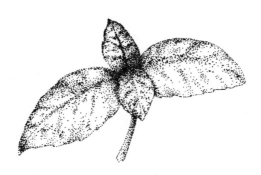

RISOTTO WITH ZUCCHINI AND JUNIPER BERRIES

Risotto con Zucchini e Bacche di Ginepro

This risotto is lighter than most risottos because it is cooked in a delicious vegetable broth, and uses olive oil instead of butter to sauté the onion. For the typical creamy taste of risotto, stir in a pat of sweet butter at the end of cooking.

◊ MAKES 4 TO 6 SERVINGS

6 cups Vegetable Broth, page 24, or low-sodium canned chicken broth

¼ cup extra-virgin olive oil

½ cup finely minced yellow onion

1 garlic clove, peeled

6 to 7 juniper berries

½ pound zucchini, smallest you can get, washed and diced into small pieces

1 thick slice (2 ounces) prosciutto, diced

2 cups imported Arborio, Carnaroli or Vialone Nano rice

8 to 10 fresh basil leaves, finely shredded

1 tablespoon butter

⅓ cup freshly grated Parmigiano-Reggiano cheese

Make broth and strain. Heat broth in a medium saucepan and keep warm over low heat.

Heat oil in a large skillet over medium heat. Add onion, garlic clove and juniper berries and cook, stirring, until garlic is golden and onion is pale yellow and soft, 6 to 7 minutes. Discard juniper berries and garlic.

Add zucchini and prosciutto and cook, stirring, 3 to 4 minutes. Add rice and cook, stirring, until it is well coated with other ingredients, 1 to 2 minutes. Add a small ladle of simmering broth and cook, stirring, until broth has been absorbed almost completely. Continue cooking and stirring rice in this manner, adding ½ cup or so of broth at a time for about 18 minutes.

When the last addition of broth is almost all reduced, add basil, butter and about half of the Parmigiano. Stir quickly until butter and cheese are melted and rice has a moist, creamy consistency. Taste, adjust seasoning and serve with remaining Parmigiano if desired.

RISOTTO WITH FRESH HERBS

Risotto alle Erbe Aromatiche

A light, delicate risotto, seasoned with an array of fresh herbs, is the perfect summer dish. The last time I made this risotto, I used basil (my favorite herb), oregano, mint, Italian parsley and marjoram, chopped them fine and added them to the risotto during its last few minutes of cooking, so they retained their color and freshness.

MAKES 4 TO 6 SERVINGS

5 to 6 cups Vegetable Broth, page 24, or 3 cups low-sodium canned chicken broth mixed with 3 cups water

3 tablespoons extra-virgin olive oil

½ cup finely minced shallots or yellow onion

2 cups Arborio, Carnaroli or Vialone Nano rice

1 cup dry white wine

2 to 3 tablespoons finely chopped mixed herbs (parsley, marjoram, basil, mint)

1 tablespoon butter

¼ cup freshly grated Parmigiano-Reggiano cheese (optional)

Heat vegetable broth in a medium saucepan and keep warm over low heat.

Heat oil in a large skillet over medium heat. Add shallots and cook, stirring, until shallots are pale yellow and soft, 5 to 6 minutes. Add rice and stir quickly for a minute or two or until rice is translucent and is well coated with savory base. Stir in ½ cup of wine and keep stirring until it is almost all reduced. Stir in remaining wine and cook in same manner. Add ½ cup of simmering broth or just enough to barely cover rice. Cook, stirring, until broth has been absorbed almost completely. Continue cooking and stirring rice in this manner adding broth ½ cup or so at a time, about 18 minutes. At this point rice should be tender but still a bit firm to the bite.

When last addition of broth is almost all reduced, add fresh herbs, butter and Parmigiano if using. Stir quickly until butter and cheese are melted and rice has a moist, creamy consistency. If risotto seems a bit dry, stir in a little more broth. Taste, adjust seasoning and serve.

RISOTTO WITH SPRING VEGETABLES

Risotto Primavera

Use whatever vegetables spring offers.

MAKES 6 SERVINGS

5 to 6 cups Chicken Broth, page 23, or
    canned chicken broth

5 tablespoons butter

1 medium onion, finely chopped

2½ cups arborio rice, page 5

1 cup dry white wine

1 cup fresh asparagus tips, smallest
    available

1 cup fresh peas or thawed frozen peas

½ cup very finely chopped zucchini

1 cup thinly sliced small white
    mushrooms

2 tablespoons chopped fresh basil

2 tablespoons chopped parsley

½ cup freshly grated Parmesan cheese

Salt to taste

Prepare Chicken Broth. Heat broth in a medium saucepan and keep over low heat.

Melt 4 tablespoons of the butter in a large saucepan. When butter foams, add onion. Sauté over medium heat until pale yellow. Add rice and mix well. When rice is coated with butter, add wine. Cook, stirring constantly, until wine has evaporated. Stir in 1 or 2 ladles of broth, or enough to cover rice. Stir over medium heat until broth has been absorbed. Continue cooking and stirring rice, adding broth a little at a time, about 10 minutes. Add asparagus tips, peas, zucchini and mushrooms. Cook about 10 minutes longer or until rice is done. Rice should be tender but firm to the bite.

Remove pan from heat. Add basil, parsley, ⅓ cup of the Parmesan cheese and remaining 1 tablespoon butter; mix well. Season with salt. Place in a warm dish. Serve immediately with remaining Parmesan cheese.

RISOTTO WITH DRIED MUSHROOMS

Risotto con i Funghi

To get the authentic flavor of this dish, use dried Italian mushrooms.

⅗ MAKES 6 SERVINGS

6 to 8 cups Chicken Broth, page 23, or
canned chicken broth

1 ounce dried wild Italian mushrooms or
¼ pound fresh mushrooms, thinly
sliced

1 cup warm water, if using dried
mushrooms

2 tablespoons butter, if using fresh
mushrooms

5 tablespoons butter

1 medium onion, finely chopped

2½ cups arborio rice, page 5

¾ cup dry white wine

½ cup freshly grated Parmesan cheese

Salt to taste

Prepare Chicken Broth. If using dried mushrooms, soak in warm water 20 minutes. Drain mushrooms, reserving liquid. Strain mushroom liquid. Rinse mushrooms under cold running water. Squeeze to remove as much moisture as possible. If using fresh mushrooms, sauté in 2 tablespoons butter until golden; set aside.

Heat broth in a medium saucepan and keep warm over low heat. Melt 4 tablespoons of the butter in a large saucepan. When butter foams, add onion. Sauté over medium heat until pale yellow. Add rice and mix well. When rice is coated with butter, add wine. Cook, stirring constantly, until wine has evaporated. Add drained dried mushrooms and reserved mushroom liquid. Stir in 1 or 2 ladles of broth, or enough to cover rice. Stir over medium heat until broth has been absorbed. Continue cooking and stirring rice, adding broth a little at a time until rice is done, 15 to 20 minutes. Rice should be tender, but firm to the bite. Stir in Parmesan cheese, 1 tablespoon butter and sautéed fresh mushrooms, if using. Season with salt.

Place in a warm dish. Serve immediately.

SHELLFISH RISOTTO

Risotto con Frutti di Mare

Prepare the fish broth a day ahead and cook the shellfish a bit ahead of time, then the cooking and assembling of the risotto will be a snap.

MAKES 4 SERVINGS

Basic Fish Broth

3 pounds fish frames (see Note below)

1 large onion, coarsely chopped

2 celery stalks, cut into pieces

2 carrots, cut into pieces

3 parsley sprigs

2 cups dry white wine

3 quarts cold water

Salt to taste

3 to 4 tablespoons olive oil

1 cup dry white wine

¼ pound clams in shells, the smallest you can get

¼ pound mussels in shells, the smallest you can get

¼ pound scallops, cut into fourths

¼ pound shrimp, cut into fourths

2 garlic cloves, minced

Pinch of hot ground chile pepper

5 tablespoons unsalted butter

1 medium onion, minced

2 cups arborio rice, page 5

1 cup dry white wine

6 to 7 cups Basic Fish Broth

2 tablespoons chopped parsley

Salt to taste

Prepare Basic Fish Broth: Rinse the fish frames under cold running water. Combine all the ingredients in a large saucepan and bring the water to a gentle simmer. With a skimmer or a slotted spoon, remove the scum that comes to the surface of the water. Simmer the broth, uncovered, 1 hour. Strain the broth into a bowl and, if you are not planning to use it right away, cool it to room temperature. It can be refrigerated for a few days or frozen. Strain broth into another saucepan and keep it warm on very low heat.

Prepare shellfish: Heat 1 tablespoon of the oil in a medium skillet with wine. Add clams and the mussels and cover the skillet. Cook until clams and mussels open, 2 to 3 minutes. Transfer clams and mussels to a bowl. Strain and reserve cooking liquid.

Wipe the skillet clean, then put it back on high heat with remaining olive oil. Add scallops and shrimp and sauté until lightly golden, about 2 minutes. Add the garlic and chile pepper and stir once or twice. Add the reserved liquid from clams and mussels and stir briefly. Return the clams and mussels to the skillet and turn the heat off.

Prepare the risotto: Melt 4 tablespoons of butter in a large saucepan. When butter foams, add onion. Sauté over medium heat until pale yellow. Add the rice and mix well. When the rice is coated with butter, add the wine. Cook, stirring constantly, until wine has evaporated. Stir in 1 or 2 ladles of hot fish broth, or just enough to barely cover the rice. Stir over medium heat until broth has been absorbed. Continue cooking and stirring the rice, adding broth a little at a time about 15 minutes.

Add the shellfish and the pan juices. Stir in the parsley and the remaining butter. Cook 1 to 2 minutes longer. At this point the rice should have a moist, creamy consistency. Taste and adjust the seasoning and serve at once.

Note

Fish frames are a mixture of fish heads, bones and fish scraps available in fish markets, sold for the purpose of making fish broth. You can assemble your own fish frames by freezing any odd pieces of fish parts.

RISOTTO WITH CHAMPAGNE

Risotto allo Champagne

Whoever created this outstanding dish deserves a toast, with champagne, of course.

၆၀ **MAKES 6 SERVINGS**

4 cups Chicken Broth, page 23, or
   canned chicken broth
5 tablespoons butter
1 medium onion, finely chopped

2½ cups arborio rice, page 5
4 cups dry champagne
1 cup freshly grated Parmesan cheese
Salt to taste

Prepare Chicken Broth. Heat broth in a medium saucepan and keep warm over low heat.

Melt 4 tablespoons of the butter in a large saucepan. When butter foams, add onion. Sauté over medium heat until pale yellow. Add rice and mix well. When rice is coated with butter, add 1 cup champagne. Cook, stirring constantly, until champagne has evaporated. Stir in 1 or 2 ladles of broth, or enough to cover rice. Stir over medium heat until broth has been absorbed. Continue cooking and stirring rice, adding broth a little at a time, about 10 minutes. During remaining 10 minutes of cooking, add champagne 1 cup at a time instead of broth. Do not add more champagne until previous amount has been absorbed. Rice is done when it is tender but firm to the bite. Stir in ½ cup Parmesan cheese and remaining butter. Season with salt.

Place in a warm dish. Serve immediately with remaining Parmesan cheese.

DANTE'S RISOTTO

Risotto Dante

Prepare the vegetables ahead and the cooking will be a snap.

❧ MAKES 6 SERVINGS

1 carrot, halved

1 celery stalk, halved

6 to 8 cups Chicken Broth, page 23, or
  canned chicken broth

6 tablespoons butter

1 medium onion, finely chopped

2½ cups arborio rice, page 5

¾ cup dry white wine

¼ pound small white mushrooms,
  thinly sliced

½ (10-ounce) pkg. thawed frozen
  spinach, finely chopped

2 tablespoons chopped parsley

¼ pound prosciutto, page 4, finely
  chopped

⅓ cup whipping cream

Salt to taste

1 cup freshly grated Parmesan cheese

Fill a small saucepan one-third full with water. Bring water to a boil. Add carrot and celery. Cook over medium heat until barely tender. Finely chop carrot and celery.

Prepare Chicken Broth. Heat broth in a medium saucepan and keep hot over low heat.

Melt 4 tablespoons of the butter in a large saucepan. When butter foams, add onion. Sauté over medium heat until pale yellow. Add rice and mix well. When rice is coated with butter, add wine. Cook, stirring constantly, until wine has evaporated. Stir in 1 or 2 ladles of broth, or enough to cover rice. Stir over medium heat until broth has been absorbed. Continue cooking and stirring rice, adding broth a little at a time until rice is almost done, 10 to 15 minutes. Melt 1 tablespoon of the butter in a medium skillet. Add mushrooms. Sauté until golden. Add sautéed mushrooms, spinach, carrot, celery, parsley, prosciutto and cream to rice mixture. Mix well and season with salt. Cook about 5 minutes longer. When rice is tender but firm to the bite, stir in ½ cup of the Parmesan cheese and remaining 1 tablespoon butter. Place in a warm dish. Serve immediately with remaining Parmesan cheese.

RISOTTO MILAN STYLE

Risotto alla Milanese

This golden risotto and Veal Shanks Milan Style, page 151, are traditionally served together.

§ MAKES 6 SERVINGS

6 to 8 cups Chicken Broth, page 23, or
    canned chicken broth
5 tablespoons butter
1 medium onion, finely chopped
2½ cups arborio rice, page 5

¾ cup dry white wine
½ teaspoon saffron
½ cup freshly grated Parmesan cheese
    plus additional for serving
Salt to taste

Prepare Chicken Broth. Heat broth in a medium saucepan and keep warm over low heat.

Melt 4 tablespoons of the butter in a large saucepan. When butter foams, add onion. Sauté over medium heat until pale yellow. Add rice and mix well. When rice is coated with butter, add wine. Cook, stirring constantly, until wine has evaporated. Stir in 1 or 2 ladles of broth, or enough to cover rice. Stir over medium heat until broth has been absorbed. Continue cooking and stirring rice, adding broth a little at a time until rice is done, 15 to 20 minutes. Rice should be tender but firm to the bite.

In a small bowl, dissolve saffron in a little hot broth and add to rice mixture. Stir in ½ cup Parmesan cheese and remaining 1 tablespoon butter. Season with salt. Place in a warm dish. Serve immediately with additional Parmesan cheese.

PUMPKIN RISOTTO

Risotto con la Zucca

Pumpkin gives a delicate taste to this risotto from Lombardy.

‖ MAKES 4 SERVINGS

6 cups Chicken Broth, page 23, or
   canned chicken broth
1 pound pumpkin
4 tablespoons butter
1 medium onion, finely chopped

2 cups arborio rice, page 5
½ cup freshly grated Parmesan cheese
   plus additional for serving

Prepare Chicken Broth. Heat broth in a medium saucepan and keep warm over low heat.

Peel pumpkin and discard seeds. Cut pumpkin into very small pieces. Melt 3 tablespoons of the butter in a large saucepan. When butter foams, add onion. Sauté over medium heat until pale yellow. Add pumpkin and mix well. Add 1 or 2 ladles of broth, or enough to cover pumpkin mixture. Cook uncovered over medium heat 10 minutes. Stir in rice and 1 cup broth. Continue cooking and stirring rice, adding broth a little at a time until rice is done, 15 to 20 minutes. Rice should be tender but firm to the bite. Add ½ cup Parmesan cheese and 1 tablespoon butter; mix well.

Place in a warm dish. Serve immediately with additional Parmesan cheese.

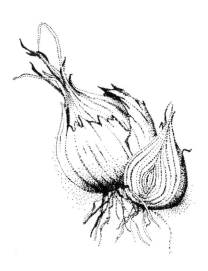

RISOTTO WITH ASPARAGUS TIPS

Risotto con Punte di Asparagi

Make this dish in the summer months when asparagus is at its peak.

MAKES 6 SERVINGS

6 cups **Chicken Broth, page 23, or**
  canned chicken broth
1½ pounds **asparagus, smallest available**
6 tablespoons **butter**
1 medium **onion, finely chopped**
2½ cups **arborio rice, page 5**

½ cup **dry white wine**
⅓ cup **whipping cream**
½ cup **freshly grated Parmesan cheese**
  plus additional for serving
Salt to taste

Prepare Chicken Broth.

Clean asparagus and cut off tips. Reserve stalks for another use.

Heat broth in a medium saucepan and keep warm over low heat.

Melt 4 tablespoons of the butter in a large saucepan. When butter foams, add onion. Sauté over medium heat until pale yellow. Add rice and mix well. When rice is coated with butter, add wine. Cook, stirring constantly, until wine has evaporated. Stir in 1 or 2 ladles of broth, or enough to cover rice. Stir over medium heat until broth has been absorbed. Add more broth as liquid is absorbed. After 10 minutes add asparagus tips. Continue cooking and stirring rice, adding broth a little at a time until rice is done, about 10 minutes. Rice should be tender but firm to the bite. Add cream, ½ cup Parmesan cheese and remaining butter; mix gently. Season with salt.

Place in a warm dish. Serve immediately with additional Parmesan cheese.

Fish and Shellfish

*I*taly is a long, thin peninsula with the Adriatic Sea to the east and the Mediterranean Sea to the west. No wonder Italians are great fish lovers! But if you leave the Italian seacoasts and go inland, you will find fish consumption is less than you would expect from a country practically surrounded by water.

I was born in Emilia-Romagna. The Emilia side is inland; the Romagna side has a sea-coast. In my family, fish was eaten maybe two or three times a month. But I would readily get into a car with family or friends and drive to the coastal town of Rimini to eat the fresh catch of the day. Everybody knew the best fish to be had was at the coast.

Restaurants of the area specialized in excellently prepared fish. Inside these restaurants, fish was generally displayed on a long table with some fish still alive inside large containers of water. You would choose the fish you preferred, then 10 minutes later it would arrive on your plate, broiled, fried, or poached.

What could be better than a fresh batch of shrimp coated lightly with a parsley-garlic mixture and broiled for the briefest time? Or a large pot of clams, simmered in a fresh tomato and herb sauce and served over pasta? Or fresh sole, cooked in a butter-lemon sauce? Italians do not camouflage fish under rich, heavy sauces, but complement them with delicate flavors.

In addition to the marvelously simple fish dishes, every coastal town in Italy has its own fish soup. Whether it is *Broeto* from Venice, *Cacciucco* from Leghorn, or *Ciuppin* from Liguria, each region claims its own fish soup is the best.

The first thing to do when buying fish is to make sure it is fresh. If fish has the head still on, look at the eyes. They should be bright and rounded, not sunken. Look for a moist, shiny skin. The body should be firm and compact, not mushy. Fish should have a fresh ocean smell. If you don't plan to use fresh fish the same day, place the wrapped fish in a plastic bag and seal it tightly. Put the fish in the coldest part of your refrigerator immediately. Use it within two days.

Frozen fish tends to lose part of its precious moisture as it thaws. This leaves the fish mushy. When you use frozen fish, thaw it in the refrigerator for several hours or overnight. Don't leave fish at room temperature or it will thaw too quickly and some of its juices will be lost.

Fish and shellfish need only a short cooking time. When in doubt, undercook fish, rather than overcooking it. If the flesh flakes easily when pierced with a fork or knife, the fish is cooked. Shellfish is cooked when it is opaque all the way through. If the center of shellfish is transparent, it should be cooked longer.

Fish is high in protein, minerals and vitamins. It is also low in calories. Unfortunately the price of fish today is considerably higher than it used to be. One way to save money is to buy when fish is in season and plentiful. Many dishes in this chapter can be used as appetizers or main courses. Some dishes, like Prawns with Tomato and Garlic, can also become a divine sauce for pasta. Serve fish accompanied by chilled white wine and you will have a perfect union.

I hope the recipes in this chapter will encourage you to try simple but exciting ways to cook fish the Northern Italian way.

WHITE FISH IN SWEET AND SOUR SAUCE

Pesce Bianco in Dolce Forte

This elegant, mouthwatering dish can be done quickly and easily with a nonstick skillet.

MAKES 4 SERVINGS

4 white fish fillets, such as orange roughy, sole or halibut (about 1½ pounds)	2 tablespoons olive oil
1 cup all-purpose flour, spread on foil	1½ cups dry white wine
2 large eggs, lightly beaten in a bowl	Juice of 2 lemons
1 cup dry unflavored bread crumbs	⅓ cup sugar
3 tablespoons butter	Salt to taste

Coat fish fillets lightly with flour, shaking off excess. Dip in beaten eggs, then coat with bread crumbs. Press bread crumbs onto fish with the palms of your hands. Set aside.

Melt 2 tablespoons of butter with oil in a large, preferably nonstick, skillet. When butter foams add fish. Cook over medium heat until golden, about 2 minutes on each side. Place fish on a platter.

Discard the fat from the skillet. Add remaining 1 tablespoon butter to skillet. When the butter foams add the wine. Cook, stirring occasionally, until the wine is reduced by half. Add lemon juice, sugar and salt to taste. Cook, stirring, over high heat about 1 minute. Return the fish to the skillet and cook 1 minute longer, stirring and moving the fish gently. At this point the sauce should have a thick consistency.

Arrange fish on serving dishes, pour a few tablespoons of sauce over each serving and serve at once.

FISH IN FOIL

Pesce al Cartoccio

Fish cooked in foil or parchment paper retains all its flavor and moisture.

MAKES 4 SERVINGS

1 (3- to 3½-pound) sea bass, striped bass or red snapper, cleaned	2 tablespoons chopped parsley
3 garlic cloves, finely chopped	Juice of 1 lemon
Leaves from 2 sprigs fresh rosemary or 2 teaspoons dried rosemary	⅓ cup olive oil
	Salt and freshly ground pepper to taste
	Lemon wedges

Preheat oven to 400F (205C). Wash fish thoroughly under cold running water. Dry with paper towels. In a small bowl, combine garlic, rosemary, parsley, lemon juice, oil, salt and pepper. Cut a large piece of aluminum foil or parchment paper to twice the size of fish. Lay fish on foil or paper. Fill fish with half the garlic-rosemary mixture. Spread remaining mixture over top of fish. Fold foil or paper over fish. Pleat edges to seal tightly. Place in a baking dish.

Bake 10 minutes per pound, 30 to 35 minutes. Place fish on a board and open foil or paper. Gently remove skin from fish. Cut top half of fish lengthwise into 2 servings and place on plates. Lift off backbone and any loose bones from fish. Divide remaining fish into 2 servings and place on plates. Spoon fish juices over each serving. Season lightly with salt and pepper. Serve with lemon wedges.

Variation

Trout in Foil (*Trota al Cartoccio*): Substitute 4 trout that have been cleaned but their heads and tails left on. Wrap each trout individually. Let guests unwrap their fish at the table.

FRIED SOLE FILLETS

Filetti di Sogliola Dorati

Sole fillets, breaded and fried lightly in butter, retain all their moisture and delicate flavor.

MAKES 4 SERVINGS

½ cup all-purpose flour	4 sole fillets
1 cup dry unflavored bread crumbs	3 tablespoons butter
2 eggs	1 tablespoon olive oil
Salt and freshly ground pepper to taste	Lemon wedges

Spread flour and bread crumbs separately on 2 pieces of aluminum foil. Beat eggs with salt and pepper in a medium bowl. Coat fish with flour, shaking off excess. Dip in beaten eggs, then coat with bread crumbs. Press bread crumbs onto fish with the palms of your hands. Let coated fish stand 10 to 15 minutes.

Melt butter with oil in a large skillet. When butter foams, add fish. Cook over medium heat until golden, 3 to 4 minutes on each side. Place fish on a warm platter. Garnish with lemon wedges. Serve immediately.

MARINATED SOLE VENETIAN STYLE

Sogliola in Saor

This is a very old Venetian dish with an unusual combination of ingredients.

MAKES 6 SERVINGS

⅓ cup raisins	2 large onions, thinly sliced
½ cup all-purpose flour	⅓ cup white wine vinegar
6 sole fillets	1 tablespoon sugar
½ cup olive oil	⅓ cup pine nuts
Salt to taste	1 tablespoon chopped parsley

Put raisins in a small bowl. Add enough warm water to cover. Let stand 20 minutes, then drain.

Spread flour on aluminum foil. Coat fillets with flour, shaking off excess.

Heat ⅓ cup of the oil in a large skillet. Add fish. Cook over medium heat until golden, 2 to 3 minutes on each side. Drain on paper towels. Season with salt.

Heat remaining oil in a medium skillet over medium heat. Add onions. Sauté over medium heat until pale yellow. Increase heat and add vinegar. Bring to a boil and cook about 1 minute, stirring constantly. Add sugar, raisins and pine nuts. Cook 1 minute longer.

Arrange fish in a single layer in a large shallow dish. Spoon onion sauce over fish and sprinkle with parsley. Cover dish. Refrigerate at least 24 hours. Serve at room temperature.

STUFFED GRILLED CALAMARI

Calamari Ripieni

When properly cooked, this odd-looking mollusk is outstandingly delicious.

§ MAKES 4 SERVINGS

16 medium (about 2 pounds total)
    calamari (squid)

2 tablespoons olive oil

1 (6-ounce) can tuna in olive oil, plus
    extra for brushing

2 garlic cloves, peeled

4 anchovy fillets

3 tablespoons chopped parsley

2 small eggs

⅓ cup freshly grated Parmesan cheese

Salt and freshly ground pepper to taste

1 cup dry unflavored bread crumbs
    mixed with 2 tablespoons chopped
    parsley

Clean calamari. Hold calamari in one hand and gently pull away tentacles. Cut head just below eyes and discard hard little beak inside the tentacles. Remove the calamari *pen*. (This is actually a piece of cartilage that resembles clear plastic.) Clean inside of the body under cold running water, pulling out viscera and any matter still inside. Wash and peel away the grayish skin from body and tentacles. (The skin will come away easily from the body but not from tentacles. If it does not bother you, leave it there because it is edible.) Pat dry skin with paper towels. Reserve 12 calamari for stuffing. Cut remaining 4 calamari and half of the tentacles in small pieces.

Heat oil in a small skillet. Add cut-up calamari and cook, stirring, 30 to 40 seconds. (Do not cook any longer or calamari will become tough.) Add calamari to the bowl of a food processor fitted with the metal blade. Add tuna, garlic, anchovies, parsley, eggs and Parmesan cheese and season with salt and pepper. Pulse on and off until smooth. Fill whole calamari with this mixture and secure the opening of each calamari with one or two wooden picks. (Calamari can be refrigerated for several hours or overnight, but they should be brought back to room temperature before grilling.)

Prepare grill or barbecue. Brush calamari with oil and sprinkle lightly with the bread crumb mixture. Cook 5 to 6 minutes, turning calamari to grill on all sides. Baste a few times with olive oil. Serve hot.

BROILED SHRIMP AND SCALLOPS

Scampi e Cape Sante alla Griglia

Whether you serve this dish as an appetizer or main course, it is equally sensational.

MAKES 4 TO 6 SERVINGS

1 pound medium shrimp
1 pound scallops
½ cup olive oil
⅓ cup chopped parsley

3 garlic cloves, finely chopped
½ cup dry unflavored bread crumbs
Salt and freshly ground pepper to taste
Lemon wedges

Shell and devein shrimp. Wash shrimp and scallops under cold running water. Pat dry with paper towels.

In a large bowl, combine oil, parsley, garlic, bread crumbs, salt and pepper. Add shrimp and scallops to mixture. Mix until well coated. Let stand 1 hour.

Preheat broiler. Remove shrimp and scallops from marinade. Gently press some extra bread crumb mixture onto shrimp and scallops. Place alternately on 4 to 6 metal skewers. Put skewers under hot broiler.

Broil 2 minutes or until golden. Turn skewers over and broil on the other side 2 minutes or until golden. Serve immediately with lemon wedges.

SCALLOPS VENETIAN STYLE

Cape Sante alla Veneziana

The Italian way with seafood is remarkable for its simplicity.

MAKES 4 TO 6 SERVINGS

1½ pounds scallops
¼ cup olive oil
2 garlic cloves, chopped

2 tablespoons chopped parsley
Salt and freshly ground pepper to taste
Juice of 2 lemons

Wash scallops under cold running water. Pat dry with paper towels.

Heat oil in a medium skillet. Add scallops, garlic and parsley. Season with salt and pepper. Cook over medium-low heat until golden, 5 to 6 minutes, stirring several times during cooking. Add lemon juice and mix well. Place on a warm platter. Serve immediately.

ᘯ

PRAWNS WITH GARLIC AND TOMATO

Scampi con Aglio e Pomodoro

You can find many different kinds of scampi in Italy.

ᘯ MAKES 4 SERVINGS

16 large prawns or 20 medium shrimp

1 cup canned crushed Italian-style or
   whole tomatoes

¼ cup olive oil

4 garlic cloves, finely chopped

¾ cup dry white wine

1 tablespoon chopped parsley

Salt and freshly ground pepper to taste

8 thick slices Italian bread

Shell and devein prawns or shrimp, and wash under cold running water. Pat dry with paper towels.

Press tomatoes through a food mill or sieve to remove seeds.

Heat oil in a large skillet. Add garlic and prawns or shrimp. Sauté over medium heat until garlic and prawns or shrimp are lightly colored. Stir in wine. When wine is reduced by half, add tomato pulp. Cook 2 to 3 minutes if using shrimp and 4 to 6 minutes if using prawns. Stir several times during cooking. Add parsley and season with salt and pepper.

Toast bread until golden on both sides. Place prawn or shrimp mixture in a warm dish. Serve immediately with toasted bread.

PRAWNS PEASANT STYLE

Scampi alla Contadina

If you have any sauce left over, cut prawns into small pieces and serve over pasta.

MAKES 4 TO 6 SERVINGS

4 medium tomatoes

1½ pounds prawns

¼ cup olive oil

3 or 4 garlic cloves, chopped

3 tablespoons dry unflavored bread
    crumbs

About 1 cup dry white wine

2 tablespoons chopped parsley

⅓ small red or green hot pepper, finely
    chopped, or small pinch red (cayenne)
    pepper

Salt to taste

Peel, seed and dice tomatoes. Shell and devein prawns, and wash under cold running water. Pat dry with paper towels.

Heat oil in a large skillet. Add garlic. Sauté over medium heat until garlic begins to color. Add bread crumbs and mix well. Stir in wine and cook until wine is reduced by half. Add diced tomatoes, parsley, hot pepper and prawns. Season with salt and mix well. Cook uncovered over medium heat 8 to 10 minutes, stirring a few times during cooking. If sauce looks too dry, add a little more wine. Place in a warm dish. Serve immediately.

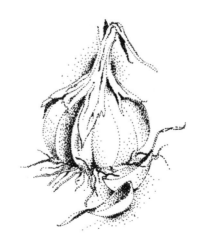

FRIED PRAWNS

Gamberoni Fritti

A crisp green salad and chilled white wine are all you need to complete a light dinner.

§ **MAKES 4 SERVINGS**

16 large prawns or 20 medium shrimp	4 garlic cloves
2 eggs	Salt to taste
½ cup all-purpose flour	Lemon wedges
Oil for frying	

Shell and devein prawns or shrimp, and wash under cold running water. Pat dry with paper towels.

Beat eggs in a medium bowl. Spread flour on aluminum foil. Coat prawns or shrimp with flour, shaking off excess.

Pour oil 1 inch deep in a medium skillet or saucepan. Heat oil until a 1-inch cube of bread turns golden brown almost immediately. Add garlic. Sauté garlic until golden, then remove with a slotted spoon.

Dip prawns or shrimp into beaten eggs. Using slotted spoon, lower prawns or shrimps into hot oil. Sauté over medium heat until golden. Remove from skillet with slotted spoon. Drain on paper towels. Season with salt. Arrange prawns or shrimp on a warm platter. Garnish with lemon wedges. Serve hot.

ADRIATIC CLAM SOUP

Brodetto di Vongole

If you like clams, you will adore this appetizing preparation. Leftover sauce should be reduced and used over pasta.

§ø MAKES 4 SERVINGS

4 pounds clams in shells, the smallest you
    can get
2 cups dry white wine
2 tablespoons olive oil
3 garlic cloves, finely chopped
4 anchovy fillets, chopped
2 ripe tomatoes, seeded and diced
¼ cup red wine vinegar

1 cup Basic Fish Broth, page 94
1 (15-ounce) can imported Italian plum
    tomatoes with juice, put through a
    sieve or food mill to remove the seeds
Salt and pepper to taste
2 tablespoons chopped parsley
8 slices Italian bread, toasted

Soak the clams in cold salted water 20 minutes, then rinse and scrub thoroughly under cold running water. Put the clams in a large skillet. Add the wine and 1 tablespoon of the oil and cover the skillet. Cook over high heat until the clams open. With a slotted spoon, transfer the clams to a bowl. Discard any clams that do not open. Strain the liquid through paper towels to remove any sand, and set aside.

Wipe the skillet with paper towels and add the remaining oil. Heat the oil and add the garlic and anchovies. Cook over medium heat until the garlic begins to color, about 1 minute. Add the diced tomatoes and cook, stirring, 2 to 3 minutes. Add the vinegar; cook until it is almost all evaporated.

Add the fish broth, the strained tomatoes and reserved clam liquid. Season with salt and pepper. Cook uncovered over medium heat, stirring, 6 to 8 minutes. Stir in the parsley and add the clams. Cook briefly until clams are well coated with the sauce, about 1 minute. Serve with the Italian bread.

Game and Poultry

*M*ost Italians are not great red-meat lovers, but give them white, tender meat, and their enthusiasms and culinary skills will perform wonders.

Most types of poultry and game, like chicken, pheasant and rabbit, have been used in Italian cooking for centuries. Turkey is the exception. It was introduced into Europe from North America by the Spaniards in the early sixteenth century.

In some northern regions, like Lombardy and Piedmont, turkey is served at Christmas. The bird is roasted and stuffed with a mixture of chestnuts, sausage, truffles, apples and prunes.

If turkey is relatively new on Italian tables, chicken is not. The chickens of ancient Rome were kept because they produced eggs. They were so scrawny that they were not considered good enough to eat. Eventually the Romans learned how to fatten chickens. They have been avidly devoured ever since. When we were children, I would often go with my brother and sister to visit an aunt who had a farm twenty miles outside Bologna. Besides climbing trees and rolling in the grass, we also chased chickens, turkeys and ducks. We would return home loaded with fresh eggs, white flour, country bread and a few live chickens. I still maintain that those were the best chickens my mother ever prepared.

The number of chicken dishes in the Italian repertory is staggering. A chicken can be broiled, baked, stewed or cooked on a spit. It can also be cooked with innumerable sauces, changing it to fit either a simple or an elaborate menu.

Chicken breasts can be used in many ways. They can be breaded and sautéed. They can be pounded and treated like veal scaloppine. Marsala wine combined with cream to make a rich sauce can turn chicken breasts into an elegant meal.

One favorite Italian way of cooking chicken is pan roasting. Using this method, the meat juices are sealed by browning the chicken in butter or oil. Then the heat is reduced and a little liquid is added to prevent the chicken from drying out.

Chicken is a particularly good buy. It is an excellent source of protein, vitamin B and iron. In selecting a chicken or turkey, look for a plump bird with firm meat. The skin should be moist but not sticky. Smell the bird. Any unpleasant odor should deter you from buying it.

In some regions of Italy, rabbit and pheasant are very popular. Rabbit has very little fat. It is delicate in taste with a particular sweet flavor. Rabbit can be cooked in many ways. My favorite method is to braise it in a rich tomato-based sauce. Rabbit cooked this way will retain all its tenderness and moisture. A few slices of steaming polenta make the perfect accompaniment.

Wild pheasant has to be caught, hung, plucked, marinated and cleaned thoroughly before cooking. But the readily available domestic pheasant can be cleaned and cooked much like a chicken. Pheasant, like rabbit, can be fried, roasted or braised. In some regions, pheasant is also cooked on an open spit, basted with lard. However you choose to cook pheasant, serve it with polenta to make an incomparable partnership.

PAN-ROASTED CHICKEN

Pollo Arrosto in Padella

Pan roasting is typically Italian and helps meat to retain its moisture.

⁊⁊ MAKES 4 SERVINGS

1 (2½- to 3½-pound) frying chicken, cut into serving pieces	2 sprigs fresh rosemary or 1 teaspoon dried rosemary
2 tablespoons butter	Salt and freshly ground pepper to taste
2 tablespoons olive oil	½ cup dry white wine
3 garlic cloves, crushed	

Wash and dry chicken thoroughly. Melt butter with oil in a large skillet. When butter foams, add chicken pieces, garlic and rosemary. Brown chicken on all sides over medium beat. Season with salt and pepper. Add wine and simmer until wine is reduced by half. Partially cover skillet. Cook over medium heat until chicken is tender, 30 to 40 minutes. Place chicken on a warm platter.

If sauce looks dry, stir in a little more wine. If sauce is too thin, increase heat and boil uncovered until it reaches desired thickness. Remove most of the fat from sauce. Taste and adjust sauce for seasoning then spoon over chicken. Serve immediately.

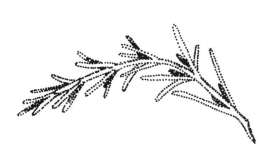

ROAST RABBIT

Coniglio Arrosto

Rabbit marinated in oil and vinegar becomes especially tender and flavorful.

MAKES 4 TO 6 SERVINGS

1 (2½- to 3-pound) rabbit

Leaves from 1 sprig fresh rosemary or 1
   teaspoon dried rosemary

4 fresh sage leaves or ½ teaspoon rubbed
   sage

2 garlic cloves

10 juniper berries

Salt and freshly ground pepper to taste

4 to 5 tablespoons white wine vinegar

½ cup olive oil

Cut rabbit into serving pieces or ask the butcher to do so. Wash and dry thoroughly.

Coarsely chop rosemary, sage and garlic together. Crush juniper berries; add to rosemary mixture. Rub rabbit pieces with rosemary-juniper mixture. Season with salt and pepper. Put rabbit pieces into a large bowl. Add vinegar and oil. Let marinate in the refrigerator 3 to 4 hours, turning meat a few times.

Place rabbit and marinade in a large, heavy casserole. Bring to a boil. Reduce heat and cover casserole. Simmer 40 to 50 minutes, stirring a few times during cooking. Increase heat to medium-high. Cook uncovered until rabbit is tender, 10 to 15 minutes and only a few tablespoons of sauce remain.

Place rabbit on a warm platter. Taste and adjust sauce for seasoning, then spoon over rabbit. Serve immediately.

RABBIT WITH WINE AND VEGETABLES

Coniglio alla Reggiana

Nothing was ever left on our plates after my mother served this special dish.

MAKES 4 TO 6 SERVINGS

1 (2½- to 3-pound) rabbit

1½ cups canned crushed Italian-style or whole tomatoes

¼ cup butter

¼ pound pancetta, page 4, cut into 4 slices and diced

2 large onions, thinly sliced

1 carrot, finely chopped

1 celery stalk, finely chopped

¾ cup dry white wine

Salt and freshly ground pepper to taste

2 tablespoons chopped parsley

2 garlic cloves, chopped

Cut rabbit into serving pieces or ask the butcher to do so. Wash and dry thoroughly.

Press tomatoes through a food mill or sieve to remove seeds. Melt butter in a large heavy casserole. When butter foams, add rabbit pieces, pancetta, onions, carrot and celery. Cook over medium heat until rabbit is golden on all sides. Stir in wine and cook until wine has evaporated. Add tomato pulp. Season with salt and pepper.

Cover casserole and cook over medium heat 30 to 40 minutes, stirring mixture a few times during cooking. Add parsley and garlic. Cook covered until meat is tender, 20 to 25 minutes longer. Place rabbit on a warm platter. Taste and adjust sauce for seasoning, then spoon over rabbit. Serve hot.

PHEASANT WITH MUSHROOMS

Fagiano con i Funghi

Serve this with a steaming hot dish of Polenta, page 86.

§◦ **MAKES 4 SERVINGS**

1 ounce dried wild Italian mushrooms or
    ¼ pound fresh mushrooms, thinly
    sliced

1 cup warm water, if using dried
    mushrooms

2 tablespoons olive oil, if using fresh
    mushrooms

1 (2½- to 3-pound) domestic pheasant

3 tablespoons butter

2 tablespoons olive oil

Salt and freshly ground pepper to taste

⅓ cup brandy

1 carrot, finely chopped

1 medium onion, finely chopped

1 celery stalk, finely chopped

3 fresh sage leaves or ½ teaspoon rubbed
    sage

2 tablespoons chopped parsley

⅓ cup dry Marsala wine or port

2 cups canned crushed Italian-style or
    whole tomatoes

If using dried mushrooms, soak in warm water 20 minutes. Drain mushrooms, reserving liquid. Strain mushroom liquid. Rinse mushrooms under cold running water. Squeeze to remove as much moisture as possible. If using fresh mushrooms, sauté in 2 tablespoons oil or until golden; set aside.

Divide pheasant into 4 pieces. Wash and dry pheasant pieces thoroughly. Melt butter with 2 tablespoons oil in a large heavy casserole. When butter foams, add pheasant. Brown on all sides over medium heat. Season with salt and pepper. Add brandy and cook until brandy is reduced by half. Add carrot, onion, celery, sage and parsley. Sauté until lightly browned. Add Marsala or port and cook 1 to 2 minutes longer.

Press tomatoes through a food mill or sieve to remove seeds. Stir tomato pulp into casserole. Cover casserole and reduce heat. If using dried mushrooms, add to casserole with reserved liquid. Simmer 50 to 60 minutes or until pheasant is tender. Turn meat occasionally during cooking. Cook uncovered 10 to 15 minutes longer. If using sautéed fresh mushrooms, add to sauce during last 5 minutes of cooking, Place pheasant on a warm platter. Taste and adjust sauce for seasoning, then spoon over pheasant. Serve immediately.

PHEASANT WITH GIN AND JUNIPER BERRIES

Fagiano al Gin e Bacche di Ginepro

Gin and juniper berries give a distinctive flavor to this succulent dish.

MAKES 4 SERVINGS

1½ cups dry white wine

2 tablespoons juniper berries

1 teaspoon black peppercorns

1 (2½- to 3-pound) domestic pheasant

Salt and freshly ground pepper to taste

6 tablespoons butter

2 carrots, finely chopped

1 medium onion, finely chopped

2 garlic cloves, finely chopped

¼ pound pancetta, page 4, cut into 4
    slices and diced

Grated zest of 1 lemon

1 tablespoon all-purpose flour

⅓ cup gin

Juice of 1 lemon

Combine wine, juniper berries and peppercorns in a small bowl. Let stand 2 hours.

Wash and dry pheasant thoroughly. Season with salt and pepper inside bird and outside. Tie firmly with kitchen twine to retain its shape. Melt 5 tablespoons butter in a large heavy casserole. When butter foams, add pheasant breast-side down. Brown on all sides over medium heat. Add carrots, onion, garlic and pancetta. Sauté until lightly browned. Drain juniper berries and peppercorns, reserving wine. Crush juniper berries and peppercorns. Pour wine over pheasant. When wine is reduced by half, add juniper berries, peppercorns and lemon zest. Cover casserole. Cook over medium heat 1½ hours or until pheasant is tender. Place pheasant on a cutting board. Combine 1 tablespoon butter and flour and work into a small ball. Raise heat. Stir gin and lemon juice into casserole. Add butter-flour ball and mix until well blended, about 1 minute. Press sauce through a sieve into a warm bowl. Cut pheasant into 4 pieces. Arrange on a warm platter. Taste and adjust sauce for seasoning, then spoon over pheasant. Serve immediately.

STUFFED CHICKEN BREASTS

Involtini di Pollo con Prosciutto e Formaggio

Fontina or Parmesan cheese paired with sage makes an intriguing combination.

MAKES 4 SERVINGS

3 whole chicken breasts

6 slices (about ¼ pound) prosciutto, page 4

6 slices (about 2 ounces) Italian fontina cheese, or 6 tablespoons Parmesan cheese

3 fresh sage leaves

1 cup all-purpose flour

1 cup milk

3 tablespoons butter

1 tablespoon olive oil

1 chicken bouillon cube, crushed

1 cup dry white wine

Salt and freshly ground pepper to taste

⅓ cup whipping cream

Skin, bone and split chicken breasts. Put 1 slice prosciutto, 1 slice fontina cheese or 1 table-spoon Parmesan cheese, and half a sage leaf on each breast. Roll up chicken breasts and secure with wooden picks. Spread flour on aluminum foil. Dip chicken breasts in milk, then roll in flour to coat.

Melt butter with oil in a large skillet. When butter foams, add chicken breasts. Cook over medium heat until golden on all sides. Add bouillon cube and ½ cup of the wine to chicken. Season with salt and pepper and cook until wine is reduced by half. Add remaining wine. Cover skillet and reduce heat. Simmer 15 to 20 minutes or until chicken is tender. Turn chicken several times during cooking. Add a little more wine if sauce looks too dry.

Place chicken on a warm platter. Increase heat and add cream. Deglaze skillet by stirring to dissolve meat juices attached to bottom of skillet. Taste and adjust sauce for seasoning, then spoon over chicken. Serve immediately.

CHICKEN BREASTS WITH MARSALA WINE

Petti di Pollo al Marsala

Elegant yet economical, this dish is an all-time favorite.

◈ MAKES 8 SERVINGS

4 whole chicken breasts	⅓ cup freshly grated Parmesan cheese
2 eggs	¼ cup butter
Salt and freshly ground pepper to taste	2 tablespoons olive oil
1½ cups dry unflavored bread crumbs	1 cup dry Marsala wine or port

Remove skin from chicken breasts. Ease flesh away from bones with a sharp knife. Cut boned breasts in half. Beat eggs with salt and pepper in a medium bowl. Combine bread crumbs and Parmesan cheese in a small bowl. Spread on aluminum foil. Dip chicken breasts in beaten eggs, then coat with bread crumb mixture. Press mixture onto chicken with the palms of your hands. Let coated chicken stand 10 to 15 minutes.

Melt butter with oil in a large heavy skillet. When butter foams, add chicken breasts. Cook over medium heat until chicken has a light-golden crust, 2 to 3 minutes on each side. Add Marsala or port. Cover skillet and reduce heat. Simmer 15 to 20 minutes or until chicken is tender. If sauce looks too dry, add a little more Marsala or port. Turn chicken several times during cooking.

Place chicken on a warm platter. Taste and adjust sauce for seasoning, then spoon over chicken. Serve immediately.

CHICKEN HUNTER STYLE

Pollo alla Cacciatora

This is the way we make this popular dish in Emilia-Romagna.

§ MAKES 4 SERVINGS

1 ounce dried wild Italian mushrooms or ½ pound fresh mushrooms, thinly sliced

1 cup warm water, if using dried mushrooms

2 tablespoons olive oil, if using fresh mushrooms

2 cups canned crushed Italian-style or whole tomatoes

1 (3- to 3½-pound) frying chicken, cut into serving pieces

½ cup all-purpose flour

3 to 4 tablespoons olive oil

2 garlic cloves

1 medium onion, thinly sliced

¼ pound pancetta, page 4, cut into 4 slices and diced

¾ cup dry Marsala wine or dry white wine

Salt and freshly ground pepper to taste

If using dried mushrooms, soak in warm water 20 minutes. Drain mushrooms, reserving liquid. Strain mushroom liquid. Rinse mushrooms under cold running water. Squeeze to remove as much moisture as possible. If using fresh mushrooms, sauté in 2 tablespoons oil until golden; set aside.

Press tomatoes through a food mill or sieve to remove seeds.

Wash and dry chicken pieces thoroughly. Spread flour on aluminum foil. Coat chicken pieces with flour. Heat 3 to 4 tablespoons oil in a large heavy casserole. Add garlic and chicken. Brown chicken on all sides over medium heat. Discard garlic. Remove chicken from casserole. Add onion to casserole and sauté until pale yellow. Add pancetta and sauté a few minutes longer.

Return chicken to casserole. Increase heat and add Marsala or white wine and cook until wine is reduced by half. Add tomato pulp. If using dried mushrooms, add to chicken mixture with reserved liquid. Cover casserole and reduce heat. Simmer 30 to 40 minutes or until chicken is tender. Turn and baste chicken a few times during cooking. If using sautéed fresh mushrooms, add to casserole during last 5 minutes of cooking. Season with salt and pepper. Serve hot.

BROILED CORNISH HENS

Pollastrino, alla Diavola

Cornish hens make perfect substitutes for the small, young chickens used in Italy.

MAKES 4 SERVINGS

4 Cornish hens	**Lemon wedges**
⅓ cup olive oil	**Parsley**
Salt and freshly ground pepper to taste	

Cut Cornish hens lengthwise along entire backbone. Open out Cornish hens until flat. Place skin side down on a cutting board. With a large cleaver or meat pounder, flatten Cornish hens without breaking bones. Wash and dry thoroughly.

Combine oil, salt and plenty of pepper in a small bowl. Brush Cornish hens on both sides with oil mixture. Place in a large shallow dish. Pour remaining oil over hens. Refrigerate 2 to 3 hours, basting several times with oil mixture.

Preheat broiler or prepare barbecue. Arrange Cornish hens skin side facing heat. Cook 10 to 15 minutes. If skin turns too dark, adjust position of Cornish hens. Turn and baste with marinade. Cook 10 to 15 minutes longer or until tender. Season with additional pepper. Place on warm platter. Garnish with lemon wedges and parsley. Serve immediately.

ROASTED CHICKEN WITH VEGETABLES

Pollo e Verdure Arrosto

Crisp chicken with roasted vegetables makes a great whole meal in a pan.

MAKES 4 TO 6 SERVINGS

1 (4-pound) roasting chicken, rinsed and patted dry

½ cup olive oil

2 rosemary sprigs, chopped, or 2 tablespoons dried rosemary, crumbled

6 to 7 fresh sage leaves, chopped, or 1 teaspoon dried sage, finely crumbled

2 garlic cloves, chopped

Salt and freshly ground black pepper to taste

1 lemon, halved

1 pound potatoes, cut into large pieces

2 large carrots, cut into chunks

2 red sweet peppers, cut into large strips

Preheat oven to 425F (220C). Put the chicken in a large roasting pan. Coat it with oil and rub it inside and out with rosemary, sage and garlic. Season with salt and black pepper. Place one half of lemon inside the chicken cavity and squeeze the other half over chicken. Roast 30 to 40 minutes, basting several times with the pan juices.

Add potatoes, carrots and peppers. Bake, basting chicken occasionally, 30 to 40 minutes longer. Chicken is done when juices from the thigh run clear when thigh is pierced with a fork.

TURKEY BREAST BOLOGNA STYLE

Petto di Tacchino alla Bolognese

From Bologna, a classic but simple dish.

MAKES 6 SERVINGS

2 pounds turkey scaloppine	½ cup dry Marsala wine or sherry
½ cup all-purpose flour	½ cup whipping cream
Salt and freshly ground pepper to taste	½ pound prosciutto, page 4, or boiled ham, sliced
2 tablespoons tomato paste	About ½ cup freshly grated Parmesan cheese
½ cup water	
3 tablespoons butter	
2 tablespoons olive oil	

Place turkey scaloppine between 2 pieces of waxed paper and pound lightly. When pounding meat do not use a straight up-and-down movement. Use a sliding action so meat is stretched more than flattened. Place scaloppine on aluminum foil. Coat meat lightly with flour. Sprinkle with salt and pepper.

Dilute tomato paste in the water. Melt butter with oil in a large heavy skillet. When butter foams, add turkey. Cook over high heat until lightly browned, about 1 minute on each side. Place turkey on a warm platter.

Add Marsala or sherry to skillet. Deglaze by stirring to dissolve meat juices attached to bottom of skillet. Add cream and stir until bubbling. Stir diluted tomato paste into cream mixture. Place 1 slice prosciutto or boiled ham over each scaloppine and sprinkle with 1 tablespoon Parmesan cheese. Return to skillet. Cover and reduce heat. Simmer 3 to 5 minutes or until cheese is melted.

Place scaloppine on a warm platter. Taste and adjust sauce for seasoning, then spoon over turkey. Serve immediately.

TURKEY STUFFED WITH CHESTNUTS

Tacchino Ripieno

You can find dried chestnuts in Italian specialty stores.

℘ **MAKES 8 TO 10 SERVINGS**

Chestnut Stuffing
½ **pound dried chestnuts**
½ **pound pitted prunes**
¼ **pound sweet Italian sausage**
¼ **pound pancetta, page 4, cut into 4**
  slices and diced
1 **cup chopped walnuts**
2 **pears**
2 **apples**
Salt to taste
⅓ **cup brandy**

1 **(10- to 12-pound) turkey**
Salt and freshly ground pepper to taste
¼ **cup butter, melted**
Leaves from 1 sprig fresh rosemary or 1
  teaspoon dried rosemary
1 **sprig fresh sage or ½ teaspoon rubbed**
  sage
About ½ cup dry white wine
⅓ **cup Chicken Broth, page 23, canned**
  chicken broth or dry white wine

Prepare Chestnut Stuffing: Place chestnuts in a large bowl. Add enough water to cover and soak overnight. Rinse chestnuts, removing any skin still attached. Place in a medium saucepan. Add enough water to cover. Bring water to a boil, then reduce heat to medium. Cook chestnuts until tender, 30 to 40 minutes. Drain and set aside. Place prunes in a large bowl. Add enough water to cover and soak 30 minutes. Remove skin from sausage and break into small pieces. Put sausage and pancetta in a medium skillet. Sauté over medium heat until sausage loses its raw color, 5 to 10 minutes. Place in a large bowl. Squeeze excess water from prunes. Chop prunes and chestnuts. Add to sausage mixture with walnuts. Peel and dice apples and pears. Add to sausage mixture. Season with salt and pepper. Stir in brandy. Taste and adjust for seasoning.

Preheat oven to 350F (175C). Butter a large roasting pan. Wash and dry turkey thoroughly. Season with salt and pepper inside bird and outside. Stuff cavity at neck end of turkey. Close tightly using thread or skewers. Place turkey breast side up in buttered roasting pan. Brush turkey with melted butter. Sprinkle rosemary and sage over turkey. Roast 20 to 25 minutes per pound, 3 to 3½ hours. Baste several times during cooking with turkey juices or about ½ cup white wine. If turkey becomes too brown, cover with aluminum foil.

Transfer turkey to a large cutting board and cool 5 minutes. Carve turkey and arrange on a large warm platter. Keep warm in oven while preparing sauce.

Remove as much fat as possible from pan juices. Place roasting pan over high heat. Add ⅓ cup white wine or chicken broth. Deglaze pan by stirring to dissolve juices attached to bottom of pan. Boil sauce until reduced to a medium-thick consistency. Strain and place in a sauceboat. Serve turkey, stuffing and sauce hot.

ϒᴗ

TURKEY CROQUETTES

Crocchette di Tacchino

A marvelous way to transform leftover turkey into an inviting dish.

℘ **MAKES 6 SERVINGS**

Basic White Sauce, page 205, made with 1 cup milk	½ teaspoon freshly grated nutmeg
3 to 4 cups chopped turkey	¾ cup freshly grated Parmesan cheese
½ pound mortadella or boiled ham, finely chopped	Salt and freshly ground pepper to taste
1 egg, lightly beaten	1½ to 2 cups dry unflavored bread crumbs
	Oil for frying

Prepare Basic White Sauce; let cool to room temperature.

Place turkey and mortadella or boiled ham in a large bowl. Add egg, nutmeg, ½ cup of the Parmesan cheese, White Sauce, salt and pepper. Mix thoroughly.

Combine remaining ¼ cup Parmesan cheese and bread crumbs in a small bowl. Spread on aluminum foil. Take a generous tablespoon of turkey mixture and form a small sausage shape. Roll in bread crumb mixture to coat. Press crumbs lightly onto croquette. Repeat until all mixture is used.

Pour oil 1 inch deep in a large skillet or saucepan. Heat oil until a 1-inch cube of bread turns golden brown almost immediately. Using a slotted spoon, lower a few croquettes at a time into hot oil. Turn croquettes. When golden on all sides, remove from oil with slotted spoon. Drain on paper towels. Arrange croquettes on a warm platter. Serve immediately.

Lamb, Pork and Variety Meats

*L*amb in Italy is synonymous with Easter and spring because these are the times it is traditionally served. Italians like to eat lamb when it is three to four months old. At that age, lamb has a tender, delicate flavor and its meat is light pink.

In many other countries, lamb goes to market a little older, at seven to eight months. It is still good at that age with a darker and well-marbled meat. As lamb gets older it becomes mutton. A whole leg of lamb should weigh four to six pounds. If it exceeds nine pounds, you are probably buying mutton.

Lamb can provide some extremely elegant dishes. Rack of lamb roasted with a tasty bread crumb coating is a treat for eye and palate. Lamb chops dipped in eggs, then coated with a Parmesan cheese and bread crumb mixture, are unbelievably succulent. A whole leg of lamb braised in a tomato-based mixture prompted one of my students to claim that although he was born and raised on a ranch and had eaten lamb all his life, this was the best he had ever tasted.

Some less expensive cuts of lamb can give you equally delicious dishes. For skewered lamb, either the leg or the shoulder can be used. For stewed lamb, the shoulder is your best bet.

Italians eat a considerable amount of pork, mostly in the form of sausage and ham. There are many dishes in northern Italian cuisine in which pork is barely visible but is vital to flavor. Pancetta, for example, plays a subtle but important role in cooking. Prosciutto, a sweet and delicate unsmoked ham, is eaten alone or as a topping or stuffing for roasts or chops.

In Italy, we have stores called *salumerie*. These are pork butcher shops, almost delicatessens, where all pork products are sold. These are the showcases for an unbelievable array of sausages, salami and prosciutti among other items. Most of these products are preserved, salt and air-cured, then aged to perfection. Some are fresh like the famous cotechino. Cotechino is a large fresh sausage, a specialty of Emilia-Romagna. It is made from pork rind and shoulder, salt, pepper and nutmeg. Try fresh sausages, fried or braised and served with hot polenta, for an unbeatable combination.

Pork chops and pork roasts are a favorite of many regions. A beautiful pork loin roast cooked with a little Marsala wine becomes a delicious and elegant glazed dish. Braise a pork loin in milk and you will have a melt-in-your-mouth delicacy. Roast pork with a little fresh rosemary and garlic and discover an unbeatable combination.

Many Italians enjoy variety meats such as sweetbreads, brains and liver. When you cook Calf's Liver in Onion Sauce, you will taste one of Northern Italy's most celebrated liver dishes.

I learned to like calf's liver as a young child. My mother would say, "Tonight we'll have breaded chicken." Only when I was older did I realize that the strange-looking chicken was liver. By then it was too late because I had grown to like it.

Liver recipes can be cooked in a few minutes. This is one more advantage of the food of Italy. It is outstanding and yet so simple to prepare.

ROAST RACK OF LAMB

Carré d'Agnello Arrosto

Serve with Baked Onions, page 183, and fresh vegetables in season.

MAKES 4 TO 6 SERVINGS

2 racks of lamb

2 tablespoons olive oil

Leaves from 1 sprig fresh rosemary or 1
   teaspoon dried rosemary

Salt and freshly ground pepper to taste

2 tablespoons chopped parsley

3 garlic cloves, chopped

1 tablespoon dry unflavored bread
   crumbs

1 tablespoon freshly grated Parmesan
   cheese

Trim all fat from lamb. Preheat oven to 375F (190C). Brush lamb with 1 tablespoon of the oil and sprinkle with rosemary. Season with salt and pepper.

Put remaining 1 tablespoon oil in a roasting pan. Place lamb in pan. Bake 30 to 35 minutes to give medium-rare meat. Bake another 5 minutes for medium to well-done meat.

Combine parsley, garlic, bread crumbs and Parmesan cheese in a small bowl. Sprinkle top of lamb with bread crumb mixture and cook 5 minutes longer. Place meat on a warm platter. Serve individual chops by cutting down between the ribs.

LEG OF LAMB WITH BACON AND VEGETABLES

Cosciotto d'Agnello alla Pancetta

This is a good way to make a leg of lamb feed a crowd.

ℰ **MAKES 6 TO 8 SERVINGS**

3 to 4 tablespoons olive oil

1 (4- to 5-pound) leg of lamb

Salt and freshly ground pepper to taste

¼ pound pancetta, page 4, cut into
    4 slices and diced

1 medium onion, sliced

2 carrots, finely chopped

1 celery stalk, finely chopped

1 cup dry white wine

1 (28-ounce) can crushed Italian-style or
    whole tomatoes

3 tablespoons chopped parsley

2 garlic cloves, chopped

Water, if needed

Heat oil in a large heavy casserole. Season lamb with salt and pepper and place in casserole. Brown lamb on all sides over medium heat. Remove lamb from casserole. Add pancetta, onion, carrots and celery to casserole. Sauté until lightly browned. Return lamb to casserole. Increase heat and add wine. Cook until wine is reduced by half. Stir in tomatoes and cover casserole.

Cook over medium-low heat 2 to 2½ hours or until tender. Stir sauce frequently and use to baste lamb. Add parsley and garlic during last 5 minutes of cooking. If sauce becomes too thick, add a little water. Place lamb on a cutting board and cool 5 minutes. Keep sauce warm. Slice lamb and arrange on a warm platter. Taste and adjust sauce for seasoning, then spoon over meat. Serve immediately.

FRIED LAMB CHOPS

Costolette di Agnello Fritte

Use very young lamb for a succulent and delicate dish.

§ᴑ **MAKES 4 SERVINGS**

8 single-rib lamb chops	¾ cup freshly grated Parmesan cheese
2 eggs	¾ cup dry unflavored bread crumbs
Salt and freshly ground pepper to taste	¼ cup butter
½ cup all-purpose flour	2 tablespoons olive oil

Trim all fat from lamb chops. Beat eggs with salt and pepper in a medium bowl. Spread flour on aluminum foil. Combine Parmesan cheese and bread crumbs in a small bowl. Spread on a second piece of foil. Coat chops lightly with flour. Dip chops in beaten eggs, then coat with bread crumb mixture. Press mixture onto chops with the palms of your hands. Let coated chops stand 10 to 15 minutes.

Melt butter with oil in a large skillet. When butter foams, add chops. Cook over medium heat until meat has a light-golden crust, 2 to 3 minutes on each side. Drain chops on paper towels. Place chops on a warm platter. Season with salt. Serve immediately.

SKEWERED LAMB

Agnellino allo Spiedo

In Italy, tender young lamb is cooked on an open spit. Broiling also gives excellent results.

❧ MAKES 8 SERVINGS

1 (3- to 3½-pound) leg of lamb

Marinade

4 to 5 cups dry white wine

2 sprigs fresh rosemary or 2 teaspoons
   dried rosemary

5 fresh sage leaves or 1 teaspoon rubbed
   sage

3 garlic cloves, crushed

4 to 5 fresh bay leaves or 1 teaspoon
   crushed dried bay leaves

1 medium onion, sliced

Salt and freshly ground pepper to taste

½ pound pancetta, page 4, cut into
   4 slices

⅓ cup chopped parsley

4 garlic cloves, chopped

¼ cup olive oil

2 medium onions, cut into large pieces,
   plus additional for brushing

3 tomatoes, quartered

Salt and freshly ground pepper to taste

Trim all fat from lamb and cut in 2- to 2½-inch cubes. Prepare Marinade: Combine all ingredients in a medium bowl. Combine meat and marinade in a large bowl; stir well. Cover and refrigerate overnight.

Preheat broiler or prepare barbecue. Cut pancetta into large pieces. Mix parsley, garlic and ¼ cup oil in a small bowl; set aside. Drain lamb and dry on paper towels. Alternate lamb on skewers with pancetta, onion pieces and tomato quarters. Brush with oil. Broil to preferred doneness, brushing frequently with oil during cooking. A few minutes before removing meat from broiler, brush lamb with parsley-garlic mixture. Season with salt and pepper. Serve immediately.

LAMB STEW BOLOGNA STYLE

Spezzatino di Agnello alla Bolognese

A loaf of bread and a bottle of red wine will add the perfect touch to this simple meal.

§♭ MAKES 4 TO 6 SERVINGS

1 (2- to 2½-pound) boneless shoulder of lamb

1½ cups canned crushed Italian-style or whole tomatoes

3 tablespoons olive oil

3 tablespoons butter

2 garlic cloves, chopped

2 or 3 sprigs fresh rosemary or 1 tablespoon dried rosemary

¾ cup light, red wine

Salt and freshly ground pepper to taste

Trim all fat from lamb. Cut meat in 1½- to 2-inch cubes.

Press tomatoes through a food mill or sieve to remove seeds (see page 207).

Heat oil in a medium skillet. Add lamb. Sauté over medium heat until lamb is colored on all sides, 2 to 3 minutes. Remove lamb from skillet.

Discard all fat from skillet and add butter. When butter foams, add garlic and rosemary. Return lamb to skillet. Before garlic changes color, stir in wine and cook until wine is reduced by half. Add tomato pulp. Season with salt and pepper. Cook uncovered 25 to 30 minutes over medium heat, stirring occasionally. Serve hot.

ROASTED LEG OF LAMB WITH GARLIC AND ROSEMARY

Arrosto di Agnello con Aglio e Rosmarino

For medium-rare lamb, cook 12 to 13 minutes per pound.

MAKES 6 TO 8 SERVINGS

1 (5- to 6-pound) leg of lamb, trimmed
   of all extra fat
4 to 5 tablespoons olive oil
3 garlic cloves, minced

2 to 3 rosemary sprigs, chopped, or 1
   tablespoon dried rosemary, crumbled
Salt and freshly ground pepper to taste
1 cup dry white wine

Preheat oven to 400F (205C). Rinse lamb under cold running water and pat dry with paper towels. Heat oil in a large heavy Dutch oven or roaster over medium-high heat. Add the lamb and brown it on all sides. Turn off the heat. As soon as you can handle the lamb, rub it on all sides with garlic and rosemary, and season it with salt and pepper.

Return lamb to pan and roast in the oven, uncovered, 1 to 1½ hours depending on desired doneness; baste with the pan juices several times during cooking. If the meat sticks to pan during cooking, add a little of the white wine. Transfer the lamb to a cutting board and let it sit about 5 minutes before carving.

Meanwhile put the pan over high heat and add the wine. With a wooden spoon scrape and loosen up the bits and pieces attached to the bottom of pan. Cook until the wine is reduced by half. Carve the lamb into thin slices, spoon a bit of pan juices over the lamb and serve at once.

Variation

About ½ hour before you remove the lamb from the oven, add some peeled potatoes, cut into large chunks, to the pan and mix them well with the pan juices. Serve them alongside the roasted lamb.

PORK AND RICOTTA ROLL WRAPPED IN PROSCIUTTO

Rifreddo Casalingo di Maiale e Ricotta

Rifreddi or galantine are meat-based preparations that are shaped into loaves or into rolls, poached or roasted and served at room temperature with or without cubes of flavored gelatin. These dishes could be as elegant or as homey as one wished. This simple version was a favorite of my mother.

MAKES 6 SERVINGS

Broth
1 small yellow onion, peeled and cut into wedges
2 carrots, cut into medium rounds
2 celery stalks, cut into 2-inch pieces
2 sprigs fresh parsley
1 cup dry white wine

Pork and Ricotta Roll
1 pound ground pork
½ pound ricotta

1 to 2 tablespoons chopped flat-leaf Italian parsley
¼ teaspoon freshly ground nutmeg
1 cup freshly grated Parmigiano-Reggiano cheese
1 large egg, lightly beaten in a small bowl
Salt and freshly ground black pepper to taste
8 slices prosciutto, approximately 6 ounces

Prepare broth: Fill a large pan halfway with water. Add onion, carrots, celery, parsley and wine and bring to a boil over high heat. Reduce heat and simmer liquid uncovered for about 30 minutes.

Prepare roll: In a large bowl or in bowl of a mixer fitted with flat paddle, combine pork, ricotta, parsley, nutmeg, Parmigiano and egg. Season with salt and pepper and mix with your hands or with paddle until ingredients are thoroughly combined. Place on a work surface, lightly wet your hands and roll mixture back and forth into a 10-inch long, 2- to 3-inch-thick roll.

Place a large sheet of foil that can be wrapped around roll comfortably on a work area, or overlap 2 regular sheets of foil to make a large one. Arrange prosciutto slices in center of foil. With 2 large spatulas, transfer meat roll over prosciutto. Wrap prosciutto around roll and tie with kitchen string.

Wrap foil securely around roll, making sure it is tightly sealed on all sides, and lower it gently into hot broth. Cover pan and simmer 50 minutes to 1 hour, making sure broth stays at a gentle simmer throughout cooking.

Using 2 large flat spatulas remove roll from pot and place on a cutting board. Cool slightly, then open foil and cool meat to room temperature. Discard foil and remove string. Cut roll into ¼-inch-thick slices and arrange them slightly overlapping each other on a large serving platter. Serve at room temperature or slightly chilled.

Variations

This pork and ricotta roll has a modest appearance but a delicious taste. If you want to make it shine, melt a few tablespoons of unsalted butter and when it foams, add 1 cup dry imported Marsala wine. Bring it to a boil and boil until it has a thick, caramelized consistency. Brush glaze over prosciutto, let it sit for a few minutes, then slice and serve.

Omit prosciutto and wrap roll tightly in foil and cook as instructed above.

~

PORK LOIN WITH GARLIC AND ROSEMARY

Arista alla Fiorentina

This Florentine dish goes back as far as the fifteenth century.

MAKES 6 TO 8 SERVINGS

6 garlic cloves, finely chopped	1 (3- to 3½-pound) boneless pork loin
Leaves from 6 sprigs fresh rosemary or	roast
2 tablespoons dried rosemary	2 or 3 tablespoons olive oil
Salt and freshly ground pepper to taste	

Preheat oven to 375F (190C). Combine garlic, rosemary, salt and pepper in a small bowl. With a thin knife, make 7 to 8 slits about ½ inch deep in roast. Fill slits with half the garlic-rosemary mixture. Spread remaining mixture over meat. Put oil in a roasting pan. Place roast in pan and insert a meat thermometer.

Bake 2 to 2½ hours or until roast reaches preferred doneness according to meat thermometer; baste roast frequently with its own juices. Place roast on a cutting board and cool 5 minutes. Slice roast and arrange on a warm platter. Serve immediately with a few tablespoons of the juices.

PORK LOIN BRAISED IN MILK

Arrosto di Maiale al Latte

Tender, juicy and delicate, this old Bolognese dish is a winner.

MAKES 6 TO 8 SERVINGS

2 tablespoons butter

2 tablespoons olive oil

1 (3- to 3½-pound) boneless pork loin
   roast

Salt and freshly ground pepper to taste

2½ cups milk

½ cup whipping cream

2 tablespoons freshly grated Parmesan
   cheese

Melt butter with oil in a large heavy casserole over medium heat. When butter foams, add pork. Brown pork on all sides. Season with salt and pepper. Stir in milk and bring to a boil. Partially cover casserole and reduce heat.

Cook pork 2 to 2½ hours or until tender; baste pork several times during cooking. If sauce looks too dry during cooking, add a little more milk.

Place pork on a cutting board. Only 1 or 2 tablespoons of thick milky sauce should be left in casserole. If too much sauce remains, cook uncovered over high heat 10 to 15 minutes. Remove as much fat as possible from sauce. Add cream and Parmesan cheese to sauce. Stir with a wooden spoon over high heat to dissolve meat juices. Put sauce in a blender or food processor and process until smooth. Return sauce to casserole and simmer until sauce has a thick, creamy consistency, 1 to 2 minutes. Taste and adjust for seasoning. Slice pork and arrange on a large warm platter. Spoon sauce over pork. Serve immediately.

Variation

Omit cream and Parmesan cheese. Cook pork uncovered during final 10 to 15 minutes over medium-high heat. Cook until all milk has evaporated and only brown particles remain in casserole.

PORK LOIN WITH MARSALA WINE

Arrosto di Maiale al Marsala

Add exciting color with Baked Tomatoes, page 180, and a green-vegetable salad.

❦ MAKES 6 SERVINGS

1 (2½- to 3-pound) boneless pork loin roast

Leaves from 3 sprigs fresh rosemary or 1 tablespoon dried rosemary

2 garlic cloves, chopped

3 tablespoons butter

2 tablespoons olive oil

Salt and freshly ground pepper to taste

1 cup dry white wine

½ cup dry Marsala wine or sherry

⅓ cup whipping cream

Rub pork with rosemary and garlic. Melt butter with oil in a large heavy casserole over medium heat. When butter foams, add pork. Brown meat on all sides. Add salt and pepper. Add ¾ cup of the white wine. Deglaze casserole by stirring to dissolve meat juices attached to bottom of casserole. Partially cover casserole and reduce heat. Cook pork 2 hours or until tender; baste pork several times during cooking. If sauce looks too dry, add remaining wine.

Place pork on a cutting board. Remove as much fat as possible from pan juices. Add Marsala or sherry and cream to pan juices. Stir over high heat until sauce has a medium-thick consistency. Taste and adjust for seasoning. Slice pork and arrange on a warm platter. Spoon sauce over pork. Serve immediately.

LITTLE PORK BUNDLES

Involtini Scappati

Pork tenderloin makes a tasty dish for family or company.

§Ə **MAKES 4 SERVINGS**

8 slices pork tenderloin, cut ⅜ inch thick	1 tablespoon olive oil
¼ pound pancetta, page 4, cut into 8 slices	2 or 3 fresh or dried bay leaves
	Salt and freshly ground pepper to taste
3 tablespoons butter	1 cup dry white wine

Remove excess fat from pork. Place slices between 2 pieces of waxed paper and pound until thin. When pounding pork do not use a straight up-and-down movement. Use a sliding action so meat is stretched more than flattened. Place 1 slice pancetta over each slice of pork. Roll up pork and secure each roll with 1 or 2 wooden picks.

Melt butter with oil in a medium skillet over medium heat. When butter foams, add pork bundles and bay leaves. Cook meat until golden brown on all sides. Season with salt and pepper. Add wine. Cook uncovered 10 to 12 minutes or until wine is almost all evaporated; only 1 or 2 tablespoons of thickened wine sauce should remain in skillet. Place pork bundles on a warm platter. Spoon sauce over pork. Serve immediately.

Variation
Substitute veal scaloppine for the pork.

STUFFED PORK CHOPS

Costolette di Maiale con Prosciutto

A rich, satisfying dish, the flavor will have your family and friends asking for more.

MAKES 4 SERVINGS

4 pork chops, 1 inch thick	2 eggs
2 ounces Italian fontina cheese or 4 tablespoons freshly grated Parmesan cheese	Salt and freshly ground pepper to taste
	1 cup dry unflavored bread crumbs
4 slices (about 2 ounces) prosciutto, page 4	3 tablespoons butter
	2 tablespoons olive oil
	½ cup dry Marsala wine or sherry

Make a pocket in each chop by cutting a horizontal slit as far as the bone. Cut fontina cheese into small pieces. Fill each chop with 1 slice prosciutto and a few pieces of fontina cheese or 1 tablespoon Parmesan cheese. Secure each chop with 2 wooden picks. Beat eggs with salt and pepper in a medium bowl. Spread bread crumbs on aluminum foil. Dip chops in beaten eggs, then coat with bread crumbs. Press bread crumbs onto chops with the palms of your hands. Let coated chops stand 10 to 15 minutes.

Melt butter with oil in a large skillet over medium heat. When butter foams, add chops. Cook until chops have a golden-brown crust, 3 to 5 minutes on each side.

Add Marsala or sherry to skillet and stir well. Cover skillet and reduce heat. Simmer 20 to 25 minutes or until chops are tender. If sauce looks too dry, add a little more wine or water. Place chops on a warm platter. Spoon sauce over chops. Serve immediately.

PORK CHOPS IN WINE

Costolette di Maiale al Vino

Pork chops cooked this way are tender and flavorful

જ MAKES 4 SERVINGS

2 eggs

Salt and freshly ground pepper to taste

1 cup dry unflavored bread crumbs

4 pork chops, ¾ inch thick

3 tablespoons butter

1 tablespoon olive oil

1 cup dry white wine

Beat eggs with salt and pepper in a medium bowl. Spread bread crumbs on aluminum foil. Dip chops in beaten eggs, then coat with bread crumbs. Press bread crumbs onto chops with the palms of your hands. Let coated chops stand 10 to 15 minutes.

Melt butter with oil in a medium skillet over medium heat. When butter foams, add chops. Cook until chops have a golden-brown crust, 3 to 5 minutes on each side.

Stir in wine. Cover skillet and reduce heat. Simmer 15 to 20 minutes or until wine is almost all evaporated and chops are tender. Add a little more wine if sauce is too dry. If too much wine remains after 15 minutes, uncover casserole for last 5 minutes of cooking. Place chops on a warm platter. Spoon sauce over chops. Serve immediately.

PORK CHOPS IN ONION SAUCE

Costolette di Maiale alla Cipolla

Onions become melt-in-your-mouth tender in this creamy sauce.

જ MAKES 4 SERVINGS

3 tablespoons butter

5 medium onions, thinly sliced

½ cup whipping cream

1 teaspoon sugar

½ cup all-purpose flour

4 pork chops, ¾ inch thick

3 tablespoons olive oil

Salt and freshly ground pepper to taste

Melt butter in a large skillet over medium heat. When butter foams, add onions. Cover skillet and cook until onions are pale yellow. Stir in cream and sugar. Cook 2 minutes longer.

Spread flour on aluminum foil. Coat chops with flour. Heat oil in another skillet over medium heat. Cook until chops are golden brown, 3 to 5 minutes on each side.

Add chops to onion-cream mixture. Cover skillet and reduce heat. Simmer 15 to 20 minutes or until chops are tender. Season with salt and pepper. Place chops on a warm platter. Spoon sauce over chops. Serve immediately.

SAUSAGE WITH FRIGGIONE

Salsiccia con Friggione

This is ideal for a carefree Sunday lunch with friends.

૬૭ MAKES 4 TO 6 SERVINGS

Friggione, page 173
1½ to 2 pounds sweet Italian sausages
1 to 2 cups water

Prepare Friggione. Wash sausages. Puncture sausages in several places with a fork. Put sausages and water in a large skillet. Bring water to a boil. Cook 10 to 15 minutes over medium heat, turning sausages during cooking. By the end of cooking time water should have evaporated leaving sausages and some of their fat in skillet. Brown sausages on all sides. Add Friggione to skillet. Cook Friggione and sausages 5 to 8 minutes longer. Serve immediately.

SAUSAGE AND BEANS IN TOMATO SAUCE

Salsicce e Fagioli in Umido

This dish brings back memories of cold winter nights when simple food brought my family closer together.

MAKES 4 TO 6 SERVINGS

1½ cups dried white kidney beans or
    other white beans
2 cups Plain Tomato Sauce, page 208
1½ pounds sweet Italian sausages

1 to 2 cups water
Salt and freshly ground pepper to taste
2 tablespoons chopped parsley
2 garlic cloves, chopped

Place beans in a large bowl. Add enough cold water to cover beans. Soak overnight.

Prepare Plain Tomato Sauce. Rinse beans under cold running water. Place beans in a large saucepan. Add enough salted water to cover. Bring water to a boil. Reduce heat. Cover pan and simmer beans until tender but firm, 40 to 50 minutes.

Wash sausages. Puncture sausages in several places with a fork. Put 1 to 2 cups water and sausages in a large skillet. Bring water to a boil. Cook 10 to 15 minutes over medium heat, turning sausages during cooking. By the end of cooking time water should have evaporated leaving sausages and some of their fat in skillet. Add Plain Tomato Sauce to skillet. Season with salt and pepper. Add cooked beans. Simmer uncovered 5 minutes. Stir in parsley and garlic. Cook 5 minutes longer. Serve immediately.

BOILED COTECHINO SAUSAGE

Cotechino Bollito

This large pork sausage is a specialty of the Emilia-Romagna region. Serve hot with mashed potatoes.

MAKES 4 TO 6 SERVINGS

1 (2- to 2½ pound) cotechino sausage

Place sausage in a large bowl. Cover with cold water and soak overnight.

Puncture sausage skin in several places with a fork. Place in a large saucepan. Cover with water. Bring water to a boil. Reduce heat and cover pan. Simmer sausage 1½ to 2 hours, depending on size. When ready to serve, remove sausage from liquid. Remove and discard skin. Cut sausage into slices.

ٮ

CALF'S LIVER IN ONION SAUCE

Piccata di Fegato alla Cipolla Fondente

This dish is the creation of a remarkable Milanese restaurateur, Gualtiero Marchesi.

℘ **MAKES 4 SERVINGS**

1½ pounds onions	Salt and freshly ground pepper to taste
1½ pounds calf's liver	Chicken Broth, page 23, canned chicken
6 tablespoons butter	broth or water, if needed
2 cups dry white wine	Fresh chervil or parsley

Cut onions into very thin slices. Cut calf's liver into very thin slices. Remove membrane and veins.

Combine 3 tablespoons of the butter, wine and sliced onions in a medium saucepan or casserole. Cook covered over low heat 30 minutes. Season with salt and pepper. Onions should be moist and creamy. If sauce looks too dry, add a little chicken broth or water. If there is too much liquid, increase heat and cook uncovered 3 to 5 minutes.

Melt remaining butter in a large heavy skillet over high heat. When butter begins to turn brown, add sliced liver. Cook, 1½ to 2 minutes on each side. Inside of liver should be pale pink.

Spoon onion sauce onto 4 warm serving plates. Arrange 2 or 3 slices of liver on top of sauce. Garnish each serving with chervil or parsley. Serve immediately.

Veal and Beef

*I*n Italy, milk-fed veal is one of the most popular meats.

Before we moved to California from New York, my husband was offered an attractive position in a renowned Midwestern hospital. We took a trip there to explore his future job and the lifestyle. The state was very beautiful and the position offered to my husband was prestigious. Unfortunately, it was almost impossible to find Italian ingredients in the area. Milk-fed veal was rarely available. My husband turned down the job. We were ready to change our lifestyle, but not to the point of changing our eating habits so drastically. Today, it is easier to find Italian ingredients and milk-fed veal there.

Veal can be sautéed, braised, fried, stewed, roasted or poached. A popular example of a braised dish is Veal Shanks Milan Style. Veal shanks are a relatively inexpensive cut of meat. When cooked by slow braising, the meat becomes tender enough to cut with a fork. If you intend to stew veal, use a less expensive cut. This usually comes from the shoulder. An excellent veal roast can be obtained from boned breast of veal. This is one of the less-expensive cuts. The veal can be stuffed and rolled, then pan roasted. The result is a juicy, tender roast. Veal can be poached to produce one of the best and most famous northern Italian dishes, *Vitello Tonnato*, Cold Veal with Tuna Sauce.

There are probably several reasons why beef is not a favorite with Italians. Whether these reasons stem from an innate preference or are the result of centuries of economic and social conditions, the fact remains. Yet, strangely enough, Italy produces some of the best beef in the world. A prize-winning beef admired by cattle raisers the world over, is the Chianina beef of

Tuscany. The best charcoal-broiled steak of Italy is found in Florence and is made from Chianina beef.

Aside from the celebrated Florentine Steak, beef in Italy is used mostly in pot roasts or stews cooked slowly with wine, herbs and vegetables.

When selecting beef, look for a rich color with marbling of fat. Marbling is important for a cut of meat that will be broiled or roasted. This cut of beef is generally more expensive but will be tender and juicy when cooked. A less-expensive cut of meat with less marbling is best for braising or stewing. The slow, moist cooking will produce tender and flavorful dishes.

When serving meat that will follow a pasta dish, try to balance and complement the two. If a rich, substantial first course like lasagne is served, the meat that follows should be extremely light and simple. Roast veal or pork, or veal scaloppine would be suitable. Even the vegetables should be served with a minimum of sauce. When a simple first course like Risotto with Parmesan cheese is served, the meat that follows can have a variety of sauces. Choose Braised Beef in Barolo Wine or Eggplants and Cutlets Parmigiana.

I hope one point will be clear from this chapter and throughout the book. A grasp of the underlying mood of Northern Italian cuisine is more important than a technically perfect execution of a recipe.

VEAL CHOPS MILAN STYLE

Costolette di Vitello Alla Milanese

Who said it takes forever to cook good Italian food? This dish proves otherwise.

§ð **MAKES 6 SERVINGS**

6 veal loin chops, ¾ inch thick	Salt to taste
¾ cup dry unflavored bread crumbs	¼ cup butter
⅓ cup freshly grated Parmesan cheese	Lemon slices
2 eggs	

Pound veal chops lightly. Combine bread crumbs and Parmesan cheese in a small bowl. Spread on aluminum foil. Beat eggs with salt in a medium bowl. Dip chops in beaten eggs, then coat with bread crumb mixture. Press mixture onto chops with the palms of your hands. Let coated chops stand 10 to 15 minutes.

Melt butter in a large skillet over medium heat. When butter foams, add chops. Cook until chops have a golden-brown crust, 5 to 10 minutes on each side. Drain on paper towels. Place chops on a warm platter. Garnish with lemon slices. Serve immediately.

VEAL SCALOPPINE WITH MARSALA WINE

Scaloppine di Vitello al Marsala

Veal scaloppine should be cooked and served immediately. Reheating will toughen and dry the meat.

§ð **MAKES 6 TO 8 SERVINGS**

2 pounds veal scaloppine	4 tablespoons butter
½ cup all-purpose flour	1 tablespoon olive oil
Salt and freshly ground pepper to taste	¾ cup dry Marsala wine or sherry

Place scaloppine between 2 pieces of waxed paper and pound until thin. When pounding meat do not use a straight up-and-down movement. Use a sliding action so meat is stretched more than flattened. Place scaloppine on aluminum foil. Coat meat lightly with flour. Sprinkle with salt and pepper.

Melt 3 tablespoons of the butter with oil in a large heavy skillet over high heat. When butter foams, add veal. Cook about 1 minute on each side. Veal should be light golden outside and pink inside. Remove veal from skillet.

Add remaining 1 tablespoon butter and Marsala or sherry. Deglaze skillet by stirring to dissolve meat juices attached to bottom of skillet. When wine is reduced by half, return veal to skillet. Mix gently with sauce. Place meat on a warm platter. Spoon sauce over meat. Serve immediately.

VEAL SCALOPPINE IN LEMON SAUCE

Scaloppine di Vitello all'Agro

This dish should be made at the last moment and brought to the table quickly.

MAKES 4 TO 6 SERVINGS

1½ to 2 pounds veal scaloppine	Juice of 1 lemon
½ cup all-purpose flour	3 tablespoons chopped parsley
Salt and freshly ground pepper to taste	2 garlic cloves, chopped
4 tablespoons butter	2 tablespoons capers
1 tablespoon olive oil	

Place scaloppine between 2 pieces of waxed paper and pound until thin. When pounding meat do not use a straight up-and-down movement. Use a sliding action so meat is stretched more than flattened. Place scaloppine on aluminum foil. Coat meat lightly with flour. Sprinkle with salt and pepper.

Melt 3 tablespoons of the butter with oil in a large heavy skillet over high heat. When butter foams, add veal. Cook about 1 minute on each side. Veal should be light golden outside and pink inside. Place veal on a warm platter.

Add 1 tablespoon butter and lemon juice to skillet. Deglaze skillet by stirring to dissolve meat juices attached to bottom of skillet. Stir in parsley, garlic and capers. Taste and adjust sauce for seasoning, then spoon over veal. Serve immediately.

WINTER-STYLE VEAL STEW

Bocconcini di Vitello all'Invernale

This marvelous stew tastes even better if prepared one or two days ahead.

MAKES 6 TO 8 SERVINGS

2½ pounds shoulder of veal

½ cup all-purpose flour

2 tablespoons butter

2 tablespoons olive oil

1 medium onion, finely chopped

1 carrot, finely chopped

1 celery stalk, finely chopped

½ cup dry white wine

1 (16-ounce) can crushed Italian-style or whole tomatoes

Salt and freshly ground pepper to taste

1 (10-ounce) pkg. frozen small peas, thawed

Cut veal into 1½- to 2-inch cubes. Place on aluminum foil and sprinkle with flour. Melt butter with oil in a large heavy casserole over medium heat. When butter foams, add veal and brown on all sides. Add onion, carrot and celery. Sauté until lightly browned. Stir in wine and cook until wine is reduced by half. Add tomatoes. Season with salt and pepper.

Cover casserole and reduce heat. Simmer 40 to 45 minutes or until meat is tender and sauce has a medium-thick consistency. If sauce is too thin, increase heat and cook uncovered about 10 minutes. Add peas and cook 5 minutes longer. Serve hot.

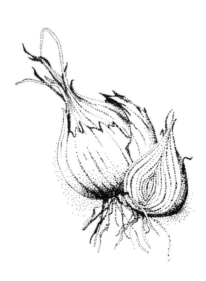

VEAL SHANKS MILAN STYLE

Ossobuco alla Milanese

The perfect accompaniment for this dish is Risotto Milan Style, page 98.

MAKES 6 SERVINGS

6 veal shanks, 2 inches thick

½ cup all-purpose flour

⅓ cup olive oil

1 medium onion, finely chopped

1 carrot, finely chopped

1 celery stalk, finely chopped

¾ cup dry white wine

1 (28-ounce) can crushed Italian-style tomatoes

2 tablespoons chopped parsley plus additional for garnishing

2 garlic cloves, finely chopped

Salt and freshly ground pepper to taste

Place veal shanks on aluminum foil and sprinkle with flour. Heat oil in a large heavy casserole over medium heat. Add veal to casserole. Brown on all sides. Remove veal from casserole.

Add onion, carrot and celery. Sauté until lightly browned. Return veal to casserole. Stir in wine and cook until wine is reduced by half. Add tomatoes. Cover casserole and reduce heat. Simmer 1½ hours or until meat falls away from the bone. Add 2 tablespoons parsley and garlic. Season with salt and pepper. Arrange veal and sauce on a warm platter. Garnish with additional parsley. Serve immediately.

Variation

Brown veal in butter. Substitute 1½ cups Meat Broth, page 22, for the tomatoes.

VEAL SHANKS TRIESTE STYLE

Ossobuco alla Triestina

When properly cooked, the meat should be tender enough to cut with a fork.

MAKES 6 SERVINGS

1 cup Chicken Broth, page 23, or canned
    chicken broth

3 tablespoons butter

2 tablespoons olive oil

3 large onions, thinly sliced

6 veal shanks, 2 inches thick

1 cup all-purpose flour

Salt and freshly ground pepper to taste

1 cup dry white wine

3 tablespoons chopped parsley

2 garlic cloves, chopped

3 flat anchovy fillets, mashed

Grated zest of 2 lemons

Prepare Chicken Broth. Melt butter with oil in a large heavy casserole over medium heat. When butter foams, add onions. Sauté over medium heat until pale yellow. Remove onions from casserole.

Place veal shanks on aluminum foil and sprinkle with flour. Add veal to casserole. Brown on all sides. Season with salt and pepper. Return onions to casserole. Add wine and cook until wine is reduced by half. Add chicken broth.

Cover casserole and reduce heat. Simmer 1½ hours or until meat falls away from the bone. Stir in parsley, garlic, anchovies and lemon zest. If sauce is too thin, remove veal and boil sauce uncovered about 10 minutes. If sauce is too thick, add a little more chicken broth. Taste and adjust for seasoning. Arrange meat and sauce on a warm platter. Serve immediately.

ROAST BREAST OF VEAL WITH VEGETABLES

Petto di Vitello al Forno con Verdure

Breast of veal is surprisingly economical and very tasty.

MAKES 6 TO 8 SERVINGS

1½ cups canned crushed Italian-style or whole tomatoes

3 tablespoons butter

2 tablespoons olive oil

1 (3- to 3½-pound) boneless breast of veal roast

1 medium onion, finely chopped

1 carrot, finely chopped

1 celery stalk, finely chopped

1 potato, peeled, finely chopped

2 garlic cloves

2 dried bay leaves

½ teaspoon whole black peppercorns

¼ pound pancetta, page 4, cut into 4 slices and diced

¾ cup dry white wine

1 teaspoon sugar

Salt and freshly ground pepper to taste

1 chicken bouillon cube, crushed

Water, if needed

Preheat oven to 375F (190C). Press tomatoes through a food mill or sieve to remove seeds.

Melt butter with oil in a large heavy casserole over medium heat. When butter foams, add veal. Brown on all sides. Add onion, carrot, celery, potato, garlic, bay leaves, peppercorns and pancetta. Sauté until vegetables and pancetta are lightly browned. Stir in wine. Add sugar and season with salt and pepper. Cook until wine is reduced by half. Add bouillon cube and tomato pulp. Bring to a boil.

Cover casserole and place in oven. Cook 1½ to 2 hours or until veal is tender; baste veal frequently. If sauce looks too dry, add a little water. Place veal on a cutting board. Put sauce into a blender or food processor and process until smooth. Taste and adjust for seasoning. Slice veal and arrange on a large warm platter. Spoon sauce over veal. Serve immediately.

COLD VEAL IN TUNA SAUCE

Vitello Tonnato

A classic, sensational dish, that is great as an appetizer or main course.

MAKES 6 TO 8 SERVINGS

1 (3-pound) boneless veal roast, from
    top round or shoulder, firmly tied

1 carrot, chopped

1 celery stalk, chopped

1 onion, sliced

2 cups dry white wine

Tuna Sauce

1 (7-ounce) can tuna fish in olive oil

4 flat anchovy fillets

3 tablespoons capers

Juice of 1 lemon

¾ cup olive oil

1 to 1½ cups Mayonnaise, page 204

Lemon slices

2 to 3 tablespoons capers

1 tablespoon chopped parsley

Trim fat from veal. Fill a large saucepan two-thirds full with water. Bring water to a boil. Add veal, carrot, celery, onion and wine. Cover pan and reduce heat. Simmer 2 to 2½ hours or until veal is tender.

Place veal and broth in a large bowl. Cover and refrigerate 3 to 4 hours.

Prepare Tuna Sauce: Put tuna, anchovies, capers, lemon juice and oil in a blender or food processor. Process to a fine paste. If sauce is too thick, add a few tablespoons of the veal broth. Combine tuna mixture and mayonnaise in a small bowl; mix well. Refrigerate until ready to use.

Cut cold veal into thin slices. Smear bottom of a large platter with Tuna Sauce. Arrange veal slices, slightly overlapping, on top of sauce. Cover veal with remaining sauce. Cover platter and refrigerate overnight. When ready to serve, garnish with lemon slices, capers and parsley.

STUFFED VEAL ROAST

Arrosto di Vitello Farcito

Prosciutto complements the flavor of veal perfectly.

MAKES 6 TO 8 SERVINGS

1 (2½- to 3½-pound) boneless veal
    roast, from shoulder, top round or
    breast
2 garlic cloves, finely chopped
Leaves from 2 sprigs fresh rosemary or
    2 teaspoons dried rosemary

Salt and freshly ground pepper to taste
¼ pound prosciutto, page 4, sliced
2 tablespoons butter
3 tablespoons olive oil
1 cup dry white wine
1 chicken bouillon cube

Ask your butcher to open the veal roast and flatten it out. It should look like a large cutlet. Combine garlic and rosemary in a small bowl. Rub mixture on inner side of veal. Sprinkle with salt and pepper. Top with prosciutto slices. Roll up veal tightly. Secure rolled meat with string.

Melt butter with oil in a large heavy casserole over medium heat. When butter foams, add veal. Brown on all sides. Add wine. Deglaze casserole by stirring to dissolve meat juices attached to bottom of casserole. Cook until wine is reduced by half; reduce heat.

Crumble bouillon cube into wine. Partially cover casserole. Cook veal 2 to 2½ hours or until tender; baste and turn meat several times during cooking. If sauce looks too dry, add a little more wine or water. Place veal on a cutting board and cool 5 minutes. Keep sauce warm. Slice veal and arrange on a warm platter. Taste and adjust sauce for seasoning, then spoon over meat. Serve immediately.

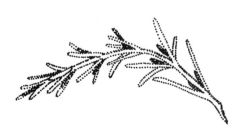

CUTLETS IN TOMATO AND PEA SAUCE

Cotolette in Umido con i Pisellini

A great dish for a cold night, dunk Italian bread or Polenta, page 86, in the sauce.

MAKES 6 SERVINGS

2½ to 3 cups Plain Tomato Sauce, page 208

6 veal cutlets

2 eggs

Salt and freshly ground pepper to taste

1½ cups dry unflavored bread crumbs

½ cup freshly grated Parmesan cheese

¼ cup butter

3 tablespoons olive oil

1 small onion, finely chopped

1 carrot, finely chopped

1 (10-ounce) pkg. frozen peas, thawed

Prepare Plain Tomato Sauce. Place cutlets between 2 pieces of waxed paper and pound until thin. When pounding meat do not use a straight up-and-down movement. Use a sliding action so meat is stretched more than flattened.

Beat eggs with salt and pepper in a medium bowl. Combine bread crumbs and Parmesan cheese in a small bowl. Spread on aluminum foil. Dip cutlets in beaten eggs, then coat with bread crumb mixture. Press mixture onto cutlets with the palms of your hands. Let coated cutlets stand 10 to 15 minutes.

Melt butter in a large skillet over medium heat. When butter foams, add cutlets. Cook until meat has a light-golden crust, 2 to 3 minutes on each side. Drain on paper towels.

Heat oil in skillet. Add onion and carrot. Sauté over medium heat until lightly browned. Stir in Plain Tomato Sauce, salt and pepper. Cook 5 to 6 minutes. Add cutlets and peas. Reduce heat and simmer 8 to 10 minutes. Taste and adjust for seasoning. Arrange cutlets and sauce on a warm platter. Serve hot.

Variation

Substitute 3 chicken breasts, skinned, boned and split for the veal cutlets.

EGGPLANTS AND CUTLETS PARMIGIANA

Parmigiana di Melanzane e Cotolette

The complete dish can be prepared a day ahead and refrigerated.

§ **MAKES 8 SERVINGS**

3 cups Plain Tomato Sauce, page 208	Oil for frying
2 medium eggplants	2 eggs
Salt and freshly ground pepper to taste	1½ cups dry unflavored bread crumbs
8 veal cutlets	1½ cups freshly grated Parmesan cheese

Prepare Plain Tomato Sauce. Peel eggplants. Cut lengthwise into ⅜-inch-thick slices. Sprinkle sliced eggplants with salt and place in a large dish. Set another large dish on top of eggplants and let stand 30 minutes. Salt draws out the bitter juices from eggplants. Pat eggplants dry with paper towels.

Place cutlets between 2 pieces of waxed paper and pound until thin. When pounding meat do not use a straight up-and-down movement. Use a sliding action so meat is stretched more than flattened.

Heat oil in a large skillet over medium heat. Add eggplants. Cook until golden on both sides. Drain on paper towels.

Beat eggs with salt and pepper in a medium bowl. Spread bread crumbs on aluminum foil. Dip cutlets in beaten eggs, then coat with bread crumbs. Press bread crumbs onto cutlets with the palms of your hands. Let coated cutlets stand 10 to 15 minutes.

Preheat oven to 400F (205C). Butter a 13 × 9-inch baking dish. Heat more oil in skillet over medium heat. Add cutlets. Cook until cutlets have a golden-brown crust, 1 to 2 minutes on each side. Drain on paper towels.

Line bottom of buttered baking dish with half the eggplants. Arrange a layer of 4 veal cutlets over eggplants. Top with half the Plain Tomato Sauce. Sprinkle half the Parmesan cheese over tomato sauce. Make another layer ending with a layer of tomato sauce and Parmesan cheese. Bake 15 to 20 minutes or until cheese is melted and golden.

VEAL CUTLETS BOLOGNA STYLE

Cotolette alla Bolognese

Fresh white truffles make this a dish fit for a king.

MAKES 4 SERVINGS

⅓ cup Chicken Broth, page 23, or
    canned chicken broth
4 veal cutlets
2 eggs
Salt and freshly ground pepper
    to taste
1 cup dry unflavored bread crumbs

6 tablespoons freshly grated Parmesan
    cheese
¼ cup butter
4 slices (about 2 ounces) prosciutto,
    page 4
10 to 12 very thin slices white Italian
    truffles, if desired

Prepare Chicken Broth. Place cutlets between 2 pieces of waxed paper and pound until thin. When pounding meat do not use a straight up-and-down movement. Use a sliding action so meat is stretched more than flattened.

Beat eggs with salt and pepper in a medium bowl. Combine bread crumbs with 2 table-spoons Parmesan cheese in a small bowl. Spread on aluminum foil. Dip cutlets in beaten eggs, then coat with bread crumb mixture. Press mixture onto cutlets with the palms of your hands. Let coated cutlets stand 10 to 15 minutes.

Melt butter in a medium skillet over medium heat. When butter foams, add cutlets. Cook until cutlets have a light-golden crust, 2 to 3 minutes on each side. Place 1 slice prosciutto and 1 tablespoon Parmesan cheese on each cutlet. If using, add a few slices of white truffles. Add chicken broth. Cover skillet and reduce heat. Simmer 2 to 3 minutes or until cheese is melted.

Place meat on a warm platter. Taste and adjust sauce for seasoning, then spoon over meat. Serve immediately.

STUFFED VEAL BUNDLES WITH
TOMATO-MARSALA WINE SAUCE

Valigini di Vitello all'Emiliana

Valigini, involtini, uccellini scappati are different names for the same basic Italian preparation. Thin slices of veal or pork are topped with savory ingredients and rolled up into small bundles. The bundles are then placed on skewers and grilled, or they are cooked with savory sauces. This version comes from my region of Emilia-Romagna. Serve with a few slices of crisp fried or grilled polenta, page 86.

MAKES 4 SERVINGS

Filling	Sauce
¼ pound sliced prosciutto, finely minced	2 tablespoons extra-virgin olive oil
2 tablespoons chopped flat-leaf Italian parsley	3 tablespoons butter
1 small garlic clove, finely minced	¼ cup finely minced yellow onion
⅓ to ½ cup freshly grated Parmigiano-Reggiano cheese	¼ cup finely minced carrot
1 large egg, lightly beaten	⅔ cup all-purpose flour
Salt to taste	Salt and freshly ground black pepper to taste
	½ cup dry Italian Marsala wine
8 veal cutlets cut from top round, about 1½ pounds, pounded thin	2 tablespoons double concentrated Italian tomato paste, diluted in 1½ cups chicken broth or water
	Salt to taste

Prepare filling: In a small bowl combine prosciutto, parsley, garlic, Parmigiano and egg; season very lightly with salt. (Keep in mind that prosciutto and ⅓ cup Parmigiano are already a bit salty.) Mix thoroughly until ingredients are combined into a nice, moist mixture. If mixture is too firm, add half of an additional beaten egg. If it is too soft add some more Parmigiano.

Place veal slices on a work surface, spread 1 scant tablespoon of filling over each slice, leaving a 1-inch border all around, and roll up veal loosely in bundles. Secure each bundle with 1 or 2 wooden picks and set aside until ready to use.

Prepare sauce: Heat oil and 1 tablespoon of the butter in a large, heavy skillet or sauté pan over medium heat. Add onion and carrot and cook, stirring, until mixture is light golden and soft, about 5 minutes. With a slotted spoon transfer vegetables to a dish.

Add remaining butter to skillet. Coat veal bundles lightly with flour and add to skillet. Season with salt and pepper. Cook over medium heat, until veal is light golden on all sides, 4 to 5 minutes.

Return vegetables to pan and increase heat to high. Add Marsala wine and stir quickly, to pick up brown particles attached to bottom of skillet. When wine is reduced by about half, add diluted tomato paste. As soon as sauce comes to a simmer, partially cover pan and reduce heat to medium-low. Simmer, stirring and basting veal occasionally, until veal is tender and sauce has a medium-thick consistency and an intense reddish color, 15 to 18 minutes.

Remove wooden picks, taste and adjust seasoning. Serve veal topped by a few tablespoons of the sauce. (The dish can be prepared completely a few hours ahead. Reheat gently before serving.)

FILET OF BEEF WITH BALSAMIC VINEGAR

Filetto di Manzo all'Aceto Balsamico

In the cooking of Modena and Reggio-Emilia, balsamic vinegar plays a very fundamental role. This is only natural, because it is in these two cities that most of traditional balsamic vinegar is made. A few drops of balsamic on a roast or a perfectly grilled or sautéed steak can enhance simple preparations to new highs. Keep in mind that the older the balsamic is, the better your dish will taste.

§ᴅ **MAKES 4 SERVINGS**

8 (½-inch-thick) slices filet mignon (about 2 pounds total), lightly pounded
⅓ cup extra-virgin olive oil
¾ cup all-purpose flour
Salt to taste
1 tablespoon butter

½ cup Meat Broth, page 22, or low-sodium canned beef broth
½ cup dry red wine
⅓ cup balsamic vinegar, or 2 to 3 tablespoons artisan-made aceto balsamico tradizionale

In a large sauté pan that can accommodate beef slices comfortably, heat oil over high heat. When oil is hot, flour slices lightly and add to pan without crowding. (If necessary brown meat in two batches.) Season with salt and cook until meat is golden brown on both sides, and pink and juicy on the inside, 4 to 5 minutes. Transfer meat to a platter and keep warm in a warm oven.

Discard some of the fat in skillet and put it back on medium heat. Add butter, broth and wine and bring to a gentle boil. Stir with a wooden spoon, scraping bottom of pan to pick up delicious bits and pieces attached to it. When sauce is reduced by about half and has a medium-thick consistency, add balsamic vinegar. Stir once or twice, pour over beef slices and serve at once.

MIXED BOILED MEATS

Bollito Misto

Serve with Green Sauce, page 206, and Sweet and Sour Sauce, page 208.

MAKES 6 TO 8 SERVINGS

1 (2- to 2½-pound) cotechino sausage	2 or 3 parsley sprigs
3 to 3½ pounds beef brisket	1 tablespoon tomato paste or 2 medium
3 to 4 large beef knuckle bones	tomatoes, quartered
1 large onion, quartered	1 tablespoon salt
2 celery stalks, chopped	1 (2½- to 3-pound) chicken
2 carrots, chopped	

Place cotechino sausage in a large bowl. Cover with cold water and soak overnight.

Puncture sausage skin in several places with a fork. Place in a large saucepan. Cover with water. Bring water to a boil. Reduce heat and cover pan. Simmer sausage 1½ to 2 hours, depending on size.

While sausage is cooking, wash meat and bones thoroughly. Put everything, except cotechino sausage and chicken, into a large stockpot. Add enough water to cover. Cover stockpot and bring water to a boil. Reduce heat. Simmer 2 to 2½ hours, skimming off surface foam frequently.

Add chicken. Simmer 1 to 1½ hours longer or until meats are tender. Leave cotechino in its cooking liquid and other meats in their cooking liquid until ready to serve. Place meats on a cutting board. Reserve broth for soups. Slice beef and cotechino sausage and carve chicken. Arrange everything on a large warm platter. Serve immediately.

FLORENTINE STEAK

Bistecca alla Fiorentina

This steak has been a specialty of Florence for centuries and is famous all over Italy.

⁋ **MAKES 4 SERVINGS**

4 large T-bone steaks, about 1½ inches thick
Salt and freshly ground pepper to taste
Olive oil

Preheat barbecue with wood or charcoal until very hot. Place steaks on grill. Cook 4 to 5 minutes on first side or until dark brown. Turn steaks carefully without puncturing them. Cook other side to desired doneness. Season with salt and pepper. Place steaks on individual dishes. Add a few drops of olive oil to each steak. Serve immediately.

FAMILY-STYLE PATTIES

Polpettine Casalinghe

Any leftover meat can be used for these crunchy patties.

⁋ **MAKES 6 TO 8 SERVINGS**

3 slices white bread
½ cup milk
1½ pounds ground veal or beef
¼ pound mortadella or boiled ham, finely chopped
½ teaspoon freshly grated nutmeg

4 eggs
⅓ to ½ cup freshly grated Parmesan cheese
Salt and freshly ground pepper to taste
1 to 2 cups dry unflavored bread crumbs
Oil for frying

Remove crust from bread. Tear bread into pieces. Combine bread and milk in a small bowl and squeeze together into a soft pulp.

In a large bowl, combine veal or beef, mortadella or ham, bread-milk mixture, nutmeg, 2 of the eggs, Parmesan cheese, salt and pepper. Mix thoroughly.

Spread bread crumbs on aluminum foil. Beat remaining 2 eggs with salt and pepper in a small bowl. Take a generous tablespoon of meat mixture, shape it into a small ball, then flatten between the palms of your hands. Dip patties into beaten eggs, then coat with bread crumbs. Press bread crumbs onto patties with the palms of your hands. Repeat until all mixture is used.

Pour oil 1 inch deep in a large saucepan or skillet. Heat oil until a 1-inch cube of bread turns golden almost immediately. Using a slotted spoon, lower patties a few at a time into hot oil. Turn patties. When golden on both sides, remove from oil with slotted spoon. Drain on paper towels. Arrange drained patties on a warm platter. Serve hot.

MEAT LOAF BOLOGNA STYLE

Polpettone alla Bolognese

It can't always be steak so let this tasty dish solve the budget problem.

✛ MAKES 6 SERVINGS

3 slices white bread

½ cup milk

2 pounds chopped beef

2 eggs, lightly beaten

½ pound pancetta, page 4, finely
   chopped

⅓ to ½ cup freshly grated Parmesan
   cheese

½ teaspoon freshly grated nutmeg

Salt and freshly ground pepper to taste

½ cup dry unflavored bread crumbs

¼ cup olive oil

1 medium onion, chopped

1 carrot, chopped

1 celery stalk, chopped

1 tablespoon chopped parsley

½ cup dry white wine

1½ to 2 cups canned crushed
   Italian-style tomatoes

Preheat oven to 375F (190C). Remove crust from bread. Tear bread into pieces. Combine bread and milk in a small bowl and squeeze together into a soft pulp.

In a large bowl, combine beef, bread-milk mixture, eggs, pancetta, Parmesan cheese, nutmeg, salt and pepper. Mix thoroughly. Shape mixture into a large flat sausage shape about 10 inches long and 3 inches thick. Coat meat loaf with bread crumbs, pressing crumbs into meat lightly.

Heat oil in a medium casserole. Add onion, carrot, celery and parsley. Sauté over medium heat until onion is pale yellow. Add meat loaf.

Bake 20 to 25 minutes or until meat loaf is light golden. Add wine. Bake 10 minutes or until wine has evaporated. Add tomatoes. Bake 30 to 40 minutes longer, basting meat loaf with tomato sauce a few times during cooking. Cool meat loaf 5 to 10 minutes before slicing. Serve with 1 or 2 tablespoons sauce over each serving.

FILET MIGNONS PIEDMONT STYLE

Filetto alla Piemontese

Some of the best truffles in the world come from Piedmont and are widely used in local cooking.

⬥ MAKES 4 SERVINGS

4 slices white bread	Salt and freshly ground pepper to taste
6 tablespoons butter	1 cup dry Marsala wine or sherry
2 tablespoons anchovy paste	⅓ cup whipping cream, if desired
1 tablespoon olive oil	10 to 12 very thin slices white Italian
4 filet mignons, ¾ inch thick	truffles, if desired

Remove crust from bread. Melt 3 tablespoons of the butter in a medium skillet over medium heat. When butter foams, add bread. Cook until golden on both sides. Place bread on a large ovenproof platter. Spread ½ tablespoon anchovy paste on each slice of bread. Keep platter warm in oven.

Remove butter from skillet and clean with paper towels. Melt remaining 3 tablespoons butter with oil over medium-high heat. When butter foams, add filet mignons. Cook 2 to 3 minutes on each side or until lightly browned. Season with salt and pepper. Add ½ cup Marsala or sherry. Deglaze skillet by stirring to dissolve meat juices attached to bottom of skillet. Cook meat over medium heat to preferred doneness.

Place a filet mignon on each slice of bread. Keep warm. Add remaining Marsala or sherry and cream, if using, to skillet. Stir over high heat until sauce has a medium-thick consistency. Spoon sauce over meat. Top with truffle slices, if using. Serve immediately.

FILET MIGNONS WITH BRANDY, CREAM AND PEPPERCORNS

Filetto con Brandy, Crema e Pepe Verde

From the Bacco Restaurant in Bologna comes this elegant, modern dish.

MAKES 6 SERVINGS

2 tablespoons ketchup	3 tablespoons olive oil
3 tablespoons Dijon mustard	6 filet mignons, ¾ inch thick
4 to 5 drops Worcestershire sauce	⅓ cup brandy
2 tablespoons green peppercorns or	½ cup whipping cream
pinch red (cayenne) pepper	Salt
3 tablespoons butter	

In a small bowl, combine ketchup, mustard, Worcestershire sauce and green peppercorns or cayenne.

Melt butter with oil in a large skillet over medium-high heat. When butter foams, add filet mignons. Cook until lightly browned, 1 to 2 minutes on each side. Remove filet mignons from skillet.

Add brandy. Deglaze skillet by stirring to dissolve meat juices attached to bottom of skillet. Add ketchup-mustard mixture and cream; mix well. Return filet mignons to skillet. Season with salt. Cook over medium heat to preferred doneness. Place filet mignons on a warm platter. Spoon sauce over filet mignons. Serve immediately.

BEEF BRAISED IN BAROLO WINE

Manzo al Barolo

This dish comes from the Piedmont region where fine wines and beef are produced.

MAKES 6 TO 8 SERVINGS

2 garlic cloves, chopped

3 to 3½ pounds beef bottom round or
    chuck

Salt and freshly ground pepper to taste

2 fresh or dried bay leaves

Pinch of dried leaf thyme

4 to 5 cups Barolo wine or any
    full-bodied red wine

3 tablespoons butter

2 tablespoons olive oil

1 medium onion, finely chopped

1 carrot, finely chopped

1 celery stalk, finely chopped

½ pound small white mushrooms

Rub garlic into beef. Season with salt and pepper. Place beef in a large bowl. Add bay leaves, thyme and enough wine to cover meat. Cover and refrigerate overnight.

Drain beef, reserving marinade. Dry beef with paper towels. Melt 2 tablespoons of the butter with oil in a large, heavy casserole over medium heat. When butter foams, add beef and brown on all sides. Remove beef from casserole.

Add onion, carrot and celery to casserole. Sauté until lightly browned. Return beef to casserole. Pour reserved marinade through a strainer over meat. Cover casserole and reduce heat. Simmer 2 to 2½ hours or until beef is tender; turn and baste beef often during cooking.

Wash and dry mushrooms thoroughly and slice thin. Melt remaining 1 tablespoon butter in a medium skillet. Sauté mushrooms over high heat until golden. Add mushrooms to casserole and cook 5 minutes longer.

Place beef on a cutting board and cool 5 minutes. If sauce is too thin, cook uncovered over high heat 5 to 10 minutes. Slice beef and arrange on a warm platter. Taste and adjust sauce for seasoning, then spoon over beef. Serve immediately.

BEEF GOULASH

Gulasch di Manzo

This Trentino-Alto Adige dish has an Austrian influence because Alto Adige was once part of Austria.

MAKES 6 TO 8 SERVINGS

1 cup Chicken Broth, page 23, or canned chicken broth

3 pounds beef chuck

2 tablespoons butter

3 tablespoons olive oil

3 medium onions, thinly sliced

2 tablespoons red wine vinegar

1 teaspoon paprika

1 (28-ounce) can crushed Italian-style or whole tomatoes

1 garlic clove

½ teaspoon dried leaf marjoram

½ teaspoon crushed dried bay leaves

Grated zest of 1 lemon

Salt and freshly ground pepper to taste

Prepare Chicken Broth. Cut beef into 1½- to 2-inch cubes. Melt butter and oil in a large, heavy skillet over medium heat. When butter foams, add onions. Sauté until pale yellow. Add vinegar and paprika. Cook, stirring, until vinegar has evaporated. Add beef. Brown lightly on all sides.

Stir in tomatoes, garlic, marjoram, bay leaves, lemon zest, chicken broth, salt and pepper. Cover skillet and reduce heat. Simmer 1½ to 2 hours or until beef is tender; stir occasionally during cooking. Serve hot.

Vegetables

*T*he Etruscans belonged to an ancient civilization that lived in northern Italy. Their love of the soil and knowledge of irrigation and fertilization made them devoted and expert farmers. The Romans inherited this love of the land from the Etruscans. They developed and enjoyed many new varieties of vegetables. Since then, agriculture has been one of Italy's national resources. Maybe that is why Italians cook vegetables better than anyone else. Their farmers have been growing vegetables longer and their produce is some of the world's finest.

One of the extraordinary sights in an Italian open market is its vegetable stalls. There you will find colorful mounds of vegetables and fruit still fresh from the farmer's patch. The Italian cook inspects all this abundance with a critical eye. She touches, smells, compares and sometimes bargains. Satisfied with her purchase, she goes home to cook the freshest possible produce.

In an Italian meal, vegetables are always present. Many times meat is omitted from a family meal in favor of one or two types of vegetables.

In selecting fresh vegetables, look for bright colors and shiny skins without bruises. A good vegetable should be firm to the touch. When selecting zucchini or string beans, choose the smallest available. Asparagus should be bright green with compact tips. Choose broccoli with tender but firm stalks and no signs of yellow flowers within the buds. Carrots should be bright orange, small and smooth. Avoid cauliflowers with blemishes and look for a compact head. Eggplants are best if they are not too large, have firm flesh and bright-green leaves. Always select mushrooms with tightly closed caps.

Use your vegetables as soon as possible after purchase to take advantage of their freshness.

Vegetables are at their best when undercooked. Prolonged cooking will result in vitamin and texture loss. Vitamin-packed vegetables are essential to good nutrition.

To serve a meal without a vegetable is almost like hanging a painting without a frame. Choose from the real-life palette of colors and you'll see that their taste and appearance will enhance even the simplest of meals.

The patient wait for seasonal vegetables becomes especially rewarding when the first tiny peas or tender asparagus arrive on the market. When buying seasonal vegetables the good cook knows she is buying the freshest and most flavorful produce. She also knows she is saving money. Once you have bought the best possible produce, very little is needed to enhance its flavor. Why cover tender green asparagus with a rich, filling sauce? Why not boil it briefly then dress it simply with olive oil and lemon juice? Or sprinkle it with cheese, dot with a little butter and broil until the cheese is melted.

Italians love raw vegetables. One of the favorite ways to eat them is dipped in olive oil and salt. What could be simpler than that? This practice must have had a humble origin, but today some of the best restaurants serve vegetables this way.

A relative newcomer to Italian cuisine is the tomato. Tomatoes were introduced into Europe from North America around the year 1500. They were treated with suspicion and used like an exotic garden plant for many years. Today we can hardly imagine Italian cuisine without the tomato. A plump, sun-ripened tomato sliced and dressed with fresh basil and olive oil is delicious.

PEPERONATA

In Bologna, Peperonata is served with Mixed Boiled Meats, page 161, and Green Sauce, page 206.

§ **MAKES 3½ TO 4 CUPS OR 8 TO 10 SERVINGS**

⅓ cup olive oil

2 medium onions, thinly sliced

5 sweet peppers, green and red, seeded, cut into strips

5 medium tomatoes, chopped

1 tablespoon tomato paste

Salt and freshly ground pepper to taste

¼ cup red wine vinegar

Heat oil in a large skillet. Add onions and peppers. Sauté over medium heat until onions are light golden and peppers have softened. Add tomatoes, tomato paste, salt and pepper. Cover and cook over medium heat 30 to 35 minutes, stirring occasionally. Add vinegar and mix well. Cook uncovered 10 minutes longer. Taste and adjust for seasoning. Serve hot or at room temperature.

BAKED ASPARAGUS WITH PARMESAN CHEESE

Asparagi alla Parmigiana

Select small asparagus with firm, tightly closed tips for this authentic dish from Parma.

჻ **MAKES 4 TO 6 SERVINGS**

2½ pounds asparagus
½ cup freshly grated Parmesan cheese
3 tablespoons butter

Preheat oven to 350F (175C). Butter a 13 × 9-inch baking dish. Cut off tough asparagus ends. Using a sharp knife or potato peeler, peel outer skin from asparagus. Tie asparagus together in 1 or 2 bunches with string or rubber bands.

Pour cold salted water 2 to 3 inches deep in an asparagus cooker, tall stockpot or old coffeepot. Place asparagus upright in water. Bring water to a boil. Cover and cook over high heat 6 to 8 minutes, depending on size.

Drain on paper towels; remove string or rubber bands. Arrange drained asparagus slightly overlapping in buttered baking dish. Sprinkle with Parmesan cheese and dot with butter. Bake 10 to 15 minutes or until cheese is melted. For a light-golden topping, put baked asparagus briefly under a hot broiler. Serve hot.

BROCCOLI WITH GARLIC AND ANCHOVIES

Broccoli in Padella con Acciughe

This is an excellent and simple vegetable dish in the true Italian manner.

჻ **MAKES 6 TO 8 SERVINGS**

2 pounds broccoli
¼ cup olive oil
3 garlic cloves, chopped

3 flat anchovy fillets, mashed
Salt and freshly ground pepper to taste
3 tablespoons chopped parsley

Cut off tough bottoms from broccoli. Using a sharp knife or potato peeler, peel outer skin. Divide broccoli and wash thoroughly under cold running water.

Fill a large saucepan two-thirds full with salted water. Bring water to a boil. Add broccoli and reduce heat. Simmer 5 to 8 minutes or until stalks are tender. Drain on paper towels.

Heat oil in a large skillet over medium heat. Stir in garlic and anchovies. Add drained broccoli. Season with salt and pepper and sprinkle with parsley. Turn broccoli gently and cook 3 to 5 minutes. Place broccoli on a warm platter and spoon over sauce. Serve hot.

FRIGGIONE

There is no translation for Friggione. The word implies a range of ingredients fried together.

MAKES 4 TO 6 SERVINGS

5 to 6 tablespoons olive oil

4 potatoes, peeled, cut into small pieces

2 large onions, thinly sliced

2 red or green sweet peppers, seeded, cut into strips

Salt and freshly ground pepper to taste

2 cups canned crushed Italian-style or whole tomatoes

Heat oil in a large skillet. Add potatoes, onions and peppers. Season with salt and pepper. Cook uncovered over low heat 30 minutes, stirring several times.

Press tomatoes through a food mill or a sieve to remove seeds. Add tomato pulp to skillet. Cook uncovered over medium heat 25 to 30 minutes or until mixture reduces to a medium-thick consistency. Add salt and pepper to taste.

BOILED POTATOES TOSSED WITH BUTTER

Patate Saltate al Burro

Many restaurants and trattorie serve boiled or steamed potatoes tossed in hot butter as an accompaniment to simple meat or fish preparations. If you are buying small new potatoes, don't bother to slice them. Simply peel them and toss them with hot butter. A bit of fresh sage can be used instead of parsley.

MAKES 4 TO 6 SERVINGS

1½ pounds new potatoes or boiling
   potatoes, washed
3 to 4 tablespoons butter

Salt to taste
1 tablespoon finely chopped flat-leaf
   Italian parsley

Put potatoes in a large pot and cover with 2 inches cold water. Bring water to a gentle boil and cook uncovered over medium heat until potatoes are tender and can be easily pierced with a thin knife, about 20 minutes. Drain potatoes and cool slightly. Peel potatoes and cut them into ¼-inch-thick slices, trying not to break them.

Heat butter in a large skillet over medium heat. When butter begins to foam, add potatoes; season with salt. Cook and stir, moving potatoes around gently with a wooden spoon, until they are heated through and are well coated with butter. Stir in parsley and serve.

SAUTÉED SPINACH

Spinaci Saltati

Serve this tasty spinach with Veal Chops Milan Style, page 148, or Stuffed Veal Roast, page 155.

MAKES 6 SERVINGS

2 pounds spinach
1 teaspoon salt
4 to 5 tablespoons olive oil

2 garlic cloves, chopped
3 flat anchovy fillets, chopped
Salt and freshly ground pepper to taste

Wash spinach thoroughly in several changes of cold water. Discard stems and bruised or tough leaves. Put wet spinach into a large saucepan; add the 1 teaspoon salt. Cover pan. Cook over medium heat 10 to 12 minutes or until spinach is tender. Drain well; cool slightly. Squeeze spinach to remove as much moisture as possible.

Heat oil in a large skillet over medium heat. Add garlic and anchovies. Sauté about 1 minute. Before garlic changes color, add spinach. Season with salt and pepper. Cook 2 to 3 minutes, stirring constantly. Serve hot.

EGGPLANTS WITH PARSLEY AND GARLIC

Melanzane al Funghetto

Capers add extra zest to this excellent dish.

৪৯ **MAKES 6 SERVINGS**

2 medium eggplants	3 tablespoons chopped parsley
Salt	2 tablespoons capers
⅓ cup olive oil	Salt and freshly ground pepper to taste
3 garlic cloves, finely chopped	

Peel eggplants. Cut lengthwise into 1-inch-thick slices. Sprinkle sliced eggplants with salt and place in a large dish. Set another large dish on top of eggplants and let stand 30 minutes. Salt draws out the bitter juices from eggplant. Pat dry with paper towels. Cut into cubes.

Heat oil in a large skillet over medium heat. Add eggplants and garlic. Cook 15 minutes, turning several times. Add parsley, salt and pepper. Cook 5 minutes longer. Taste and adjust for seasoning. Serve hot or at room temperature.

BAKED STUFFED ZUCCHINI

Zucchine Ripiene al Forno

Stuffed zucchini are excellent, but filling. Serve them with a plain roast or as a luncheon.

⁏ MAKES 6 SERVINGS

8 to 10 medium, firm zucchini

White Sauce
2 tablespoons butter
2 tablespoons all-purpose flour
1 cup hot milk
½ teaspoon grated nutmeg
3 tablespoons freshly grated Parmesan
   cheese
Salt to taste

3 tablespoons chopped parsley
¼ pound mortadella or boiled ham,
   chopped
2 tablespoons fresh unflavored bread
   crumbs
Salt and freshly ground pepper to taste
2 tablespoons freshly grated Parmesan
   cheese

Preheat oven to 350F (175C). Butter a 13 × 9-inch baking dish. Wash zucchini. Fill a medium saucepan two-thirds full with salted water. Bring water to a boil. Add zucchini. Cook over medium heat 5 to 10 minutes, depending on size. Zucchini should be barely tender. Drain. Rinse under cold running water. Pat dry with paper towels.

Prepare White Sauce: Melt butter in a medium saucepan. When butter foams, whisk in flour. Cook over medium heat 2 or 3 minutes. Do not let flour brown. Whisk in hot milk quickly to prevent lumps. Cook sauce 2 to 3 minutes longer, whisking constantly. Add nutmeg, Parmesan cheese and salt; blend well. Sauce should have a medium-thick consistency.

Trim ends off zucchini and slice zucchini in half lengthwise. Scoop out pulp with a small spoon. Combine zucchini pulp, parsley, mortadella or ham, bread crumbs, salt and pepper in a medium bowl. Add White Sauce; mix well. Taste and adjust for seasoning.

Fill zucchini shells with pulp mixture and sprinkle with Parmesan cheese. Place stuffed zucchini in buttered baking dish. Bake 20 to 25 minutes or until zucchini have a light-golden crust. Serve hot.

ZUCCHINI WITH VINEGAR

Zucchine Fritte all'Aceto

This is the vegetable dish that won the hearts of my students.

❧ MAKES 4 TO 6 SERVINGS

1½ pounds zucchini, smallest available

Oil for frying

1 cup all-purpose flour

Salt and freshly ground pepper to taste

3 tablespoons red wine vinegar

Wash and dry zucchini. Trim ends. Slice zucchini into ¼-inch-thick rounds.

Pour oil 1 inch deep in a large saucepan. Heat oil until a 1-inch cube of bread turns golden brown almost immediately. Place zucchini slices a few at a time in a sieve and sprinkle with flour. Shake off excess flour. Using a slotted spoon, lower zucchini into hot oil. When golden on both sides, remove from oil with slotted spoon. Drain on paper towels.

When all zucchini are cooked, place in a salad bowl. Season with salt and pepper and add vinegar. Toss gently. Serve at room temperature.

ZUCCHINI IN BATTER

Zucchine Fritte con la Pastella

Serve this crunchy vegetable dish with fried meats or roasts.

§ **MAKES 6 TO 8 SERVINGS**

1½ pounds zucchini, smallest available	Oil for frying
2 cups water	Salt to taste
2 cups all-purpose flour	

Wash and dry zucchini. Trim ends. Cut zucchini into sticks 2 inches long and ½ inch thick.

Put water in a medium bowl. Gradually sift flour into water, beating constantly. Batter should have the consistency of mayonnaise. If too thin, add a little more flour, if too thick, add more water. Batter can be prepared a few hours ahead.

Pour oil 2 inches deep in a large saucepan or deep-fryer. Heat oil to 375F (190C) or until a 1-inch cube of bread turns golden brown almost immediately. Dip zucchini sticks into batter. Using a slotted spoon, lower zucchini sticks a few at a time into hot oil. When golden on all sides, remove from oil with slotted spoon. Drain on paper towels.

Arrange drained zucchini on a warm platter and season with salt. Serve hot.

MUSHROOMS WITH MARSALA WINE AND CREAM

Funghi con Marsala e Panna

The look and aroma of these mushrooms are mouthwatering.

§ **MAKES 8 SERVINGS**

3 pounds small white mushrooms	½ cup dry Marsala wine or cream sherry
3 tablespoons butter	½ cup whipping cream
1 tablespoon olive oil	Salt and freshly ground pepper to taste

Wash and dry mushrooms thoroughly and cut into slices. Melt butter with oil in a large skillet. When butter foams, add mushrooms. Sauté over high heat until golden. Stir in Marsala or sherry. Cook over high heat until liquid is reduced by half, stirring occasionally. Add cream and cook a few minutes longer. Season with salt and pepper. Serve hot.

MUSHROOMS WITH PARSLEY AND GARLIC

Funghi Triffolati

Serve this with other vegetable dishes for an unusual appetizer.

MAKES 6 TO 8 SERVINGS

1½ pounds small white mushrooms	¼ cup chopped parsley
2 tablespoons butter	3 garlic cloves, chopped
2 tablespoons olive oil	Salt and freshly ground pepper to taste

Wash and dry mushrooms thoroughly and cut into slices. Melt butter with oil in a large skillet over high heat. When butter foams, add mushrooms. Sauté until golden. Add parsley, garlic, salt and pepper; cook 1 minute longer. Taste and adjust for seasoning. Serve hot or at room temperature.

BAKED TOMATOES

Pomodori al Forno

This is a colorful accompaniment for a simple fish dish.

❧ MAKES 6 TO 8 SERVINGS

6 tomatoes	2 tablespoons capers
⅓ cup plus 2 tablespoons olive oil	⅓ cup freshly grated Parmesan cheese
¼ cup chopped parsley	⅓ cup dry unflavored bread crumbs
2 garlic cloves, chopped	Salt and freshly ground pepper to taste

Preheat oven to 350F (175C). Wash and dry tomatoes. Cut in half. Using a small spoon, remove seeds from tomatoes. Drain tomatoes cut side down on paper towels 15 to 20 minutes.

Combine ⅓ cup oil, parsley, garlic, capers, Parmesan cheese, bread crumbs, salt and pepper in a medium bowl. Divide mixture between tomato halves. Place tomatoes in a 13 × 9-inch baking dish.

Spoon 2 tablespoons oil over tops of tomatoes into dish. Bake 25 to 30 minutes or until filling is crisp and golden. Serve hot.

BRAISED CURLY CABBAGE

Verze Affogate

A tasty winter vegetable, it is perfect with Pork Loin with Garlic and Rosemary, page 137.

❧ MAKES 6 TO 8 SERVINGS

1 (2-pound) curly cabbage	1 sprig fresh rosemary or 1 teaspoon
3 tablespoons olive oil	dried rosemary
¼ pound pancetta, page 4, cut into	Salt and freshly ground pepper to taste
4 slices and diced	½ cup dry white wine
2 garlic cloves, crushed	

Wash and dry cabbage; shred.

Heat oil in a large skillet over medium heat. Add pancetta, garlic and rosemary. Sauté until lightly browned. Stir in cabbage and season with salt and pepper. Cover skillet and reduce heat. Simmer 20 minutes, stirring a few times during cooking. Add wine and simmer uncovered 15 minutes longer. Serve hot.

॰ॐ

RED CABBAGE WITH SMOKED HAM AND APPLES

Cavolo Rosso con Prosciutto Affumicato e Mele

This dish comes from Trentino-Alto Adige where smoked meat is a main ingredient in local cooking.

§๑ **MAKES 6 TO 8 SERVINGS**

1 (2- to 2½-pound) red cabbage	¼ pound smoked ham, chopped
2 tablespoons butter	1 cup red wine
2 tablespoons olive oil	2 apples, peeled, diced
1 large onion, thinly sliced	Salt and freshly ground pepper to taste

Remove bruised outer leaves from cabbage. Cut cabbage into thin slices.

Melt butter with oil in a large skillet over medium heat. When butter foams, add onion. Sauté until pale yellow. Add ham and cabbage. Cook uncovered over high heat 10 minutes.

Add wine. Cook until wine is reduced by half. Add apples and season with salt and pepper. Reduce heat to medium. Cover and cook 10 minutes longer. Serve warm.

CAULIFLOWER IN BATTER

Cavolfiore Fritto con la Pastella

Vegetables fried in this flour and water batter are crisp and light.

MAKES 6 TO 8 SERVINGS

1 (2½- to 3-pound) cauliflower	2 eggs, lightly beaten
1½ cups water	Oil for frying
2 cups all-purpose flour	Salt to taste

Remove leaves from cauliflower. Slice cauliflower in half. Fill a large saucepan two-thirds full with salted water. Bring water to a boil. Add cauliflower. Cook over high heat 15 to 20 minutes or until tender. Drain on paper towels; cool.

Put 1½ cups water in a medium bowl. Gradually sift flour into water, beating constantly. Beat in eggs. Batter should be the consistency of mayonnaise. Batter can be prepared a few hours ahead.

Pour oil 2 inches deep in a large saucepan or deep-fryer. Heat oil to 375F (190C) or until a 1-inch cube of bread turns golden brown almost immediately. Detach florets from cauliflower. Dip florets into batter. Using a slotted spoon, lower a few at a time into hot oil. Turn cauliflower. When golden on all sides, remove from oil with slotted spoon. Drain on paper towels.

Arrange drained cauliflower on a warm platter and season with salt. Serve hot.

BAKED FENNEL WITH BUTTER AND CHEESE

Finocchi al Forno con Burro e Formaggio

If you have never tasted fennel, be adventurous and try this dish.

MAKES 6 TO 8 SERVINGS

4 large fennel bulbs	¼ cup butter
Salt and freshly ground pepper to taste	⅓ cup freshly grated Parmesan cheese

Preheat oven to 350F (175C). Butter a 13 × 9-inch baking dish. Cut off long stalks and bruised leaves from fennels. Slice end off bulbous base. Wash fennels thoroughly. Cut into quarters.

Fill a large saucepan two-thirds full with water. Bring water to a boil. Add fennels. Cook over high heat 10 to 15 minutes or until tender but firm. Drain fennels on paper towels.

Arrange fennel pieces slightly overlapping in buttered baking dish. Season with salt and pepper. Dot generously with butter and sprinkle with Parmesan cheese. Bake 15 minutes or until fennel is tender and cheese is melted. Serve hot.

ꝛ

BAKED ONIONS

Cipolle al Forno

These refreshingly light onions are perfect for lamb and pork roasts.

MAKES 4 SERVINGS

5 tablespoons olive oil
4 large yellow onions
Salt and freshly ground pepper to taste

Preheat oven to 375F (190C). Put 3 tablespoons of the oil in an 11 × 7-inch baking dish. Cut onions in half horizontally and place cut side up in baking dish. Season with salt and pepper. Drizzle remaining oil over each onion. Bake 40 to 60 minutes, depending on size. Onion tops should be light golden. Serve hot.

SWEET AND SOUR LITTLE ONIONS

Cipolline Agro-Dolci

These onions are the ideal accompaniment to any roast.

❧ MAKES 8 TO 10 SERVINGS

3 (10-ounce) or 2 (16-ounce) pkgs.
    frozen little onions, thawed
¼ cup butter

¼ cup packed brown sugar
¼ cup red wine vinegar
Salt to taste

Drain onions thoroughly on paper towels. Melt butter in a large skillet over medium heat. When butter foams, add drained onions. Sauté until onions begin to color, 5 to 8 minutes. Add brown sugar and stir to coat onions. Add vinegar and salt. Cook 2 to 3 minutes longer. Sauce should be thick and coat onions. Serve hot.

PEAS WITH PROSCIUTTO

Piselli al Prosciutto

Peas cooked this way also make a marvelous, light sauce for noodles.

❧ MAKES 6 TO 8 SERVINGS

1 cup Chicken Broth, page 23, or canned
    chicken broth
3 pounds fresh peas or 3 (10-ounce)
    pkgs. frozen small peas, thawed

3 tablespoons olive oil
1 medium onion, thinly sliced
¼ pound prosciutto, page 4, diced
Salt and freshly ground pepper to taste

Prepare Chicken Broth. Shell fresh peas. Bring broth to a boil in a medium saucepan. Add peas. Cook 5 to 10 minutes, depending on size. Drain peas.

Heat oil in a small skillet over medium heat. Add onion. Sauté until pale yellow. Add prosciutto and peas. Sauté 3 to 4 minutes. Season with salt and pepper. Serve hot.

STUFFED ARTICHOKES

Carciofi Ripieni

It takes a little time and patience to prepare these artichokes but they are well worth it.

MAKES 4 SERVINGS

4 large artichokes	**⅓ cup chopped parsley**
1 lemon	**3 garlic cloves, chopped**
4 slices white bread	**Salt and freshly ground pepper to taste**
½ cup plus 3 to 4 tablespoons olive oil	**Water**

Cut off artichoke stems; slice and reserve. Remove and discard hard outer leaves of artichokes. Cut sharp tips off remaining leaves with scissors. Slice off about ½ inch from top end of each artichoke. Open artichokes gently with your hands. Remove fuzzy chokes with a knife or melon baller. Wash artichokes under cold running water.

Slice lemon in half and rub over cut tops of artichokes. Set artichokes with cut part down on paper towels.

Remove crusts from bread. Chop bread into small pieces and place in a medium bowl. Add ½ cup oil, parsley and garlic and season salt and pepper. Mix well. Arrange mixture between artichoke leaves and in centers.

Place artichokes and reserved stems in a large saucepan. Pour water about 1 inch deep in pan. Add 3 to 4 tablespoons oil. Bring water to a boil. Reduce heat to medium and cover pan. Cook artichokes 40 to 60 minutes, depending on size. If water evaporates, add a little more. There should be 4 to 5 tablespoons of sauce left in pan. If too much liquid is left, uncover pan and boil liquid down. Spoon sauce over artichokes and stems. Serve hot.

ROASTED POTATO BALLS

Patatine Arrosto

These potatoes are beautiful to look at and delicious to eat.

§∂ **MAKES 4 TO 6 SERVINGS**

8 large Idaho potatoes, peeled

2 tablespoons butter

2 tablespoons olive oil

2 sprigs fresh rosemary or 2 teaspoons
   dried rosemary

2 garlic cloves

Salt and freshly ground pepper to taste

Using a melon baller, scoop potatoes into balls. Fill a large saucepan half full with salted water. Bring water to a boil. Add potato balls and boil 1 minute. Drain on paper towels.

Melt butter with oil in a large skillet over medium heat. When butter foams, add drained potatoes, rosemary and garlic and season with salt and pepper. Cook, turning frequently. When potatoes are golden, remove garlic and fresh rosemary, if using. Serve immediately.

ᘓ

POTATO CAKE

Pinza di Patate

This is a different but delicious way to serve potatoes.

§∂ **MAKES 6 TO 8 SERVINGS**

8 large Idaho potatoes

3 eggs

Salt to taste

3 tablespoons butter, melted

3 tablespoons olive oil

⅓ cup freshly grated Parmesan cheese

2 tablespoons all-purpose flour

1 egg yolk, lightly beaten

Preheat oven to 350F (175C). Butter an 8-inch-round cake pan with a removable bottom.

Fill a large saucepan two-thirds full with water. Add potatoes. Bring to a boil. Boil gently until potatoes are tender. Peel and mash potatoes while hot.

Beat 3 eggs with salt in a large bowl. Beat in melted butter and oil. Add mashed potatoes, Parmesan cheese and flour; mix well.

Put potato mixture into buttered pan and smooth top with a spatula. Brush top with beaten egg yolk. Bake 20 to 25 minutes or until top is golden. Unmold potato cake and place on a warm platter. Serve immediately.

Salads

I am always mystified when people ask me how much garlic or how many herbs I put in my salad dressing. I suppose the false notion that Italian salad dressing should contain every possible herb and seasoning started with the television commercials that advertise bottled or packaged dressing. Nothing could be simpler, tastier and less complicated than an Italian salad dressing. There is never any discussion among Italians on how to dress a salad. It is and always has been a combination of salt, olive oil and wine vinegar. But if you prefer, pepper can be added and lemon juice can replace vinegar.

Often my students want to know exactly how much oil and vinegar to put in a dressing. The amount will depend on the quantity and kind of salad. As a general rule, be generous with olive oil but stingy with vinegar. Don't forget to taste the dressing before adding it to your salad. I can give you as many proportions of salad dressing as there are salads. But, ultimately, you have to decide. Basically it is the same concept that guides all Italian cooking, whether you come from Veneto or Sicily. The best and freshest ingredients should stand on their own merits. A green or mixed salad needs only excellent olive oil and good wine vinegar to be outstanding.

Salad in Italy is never served before the first course. It is always served after the main course. There are at least two reasons for this. Salad is meant to clean and refresh the palate for cheese, fruit or dessert that follows. Another reason is that the sharpness of the vinegar used in salad dressing would destroy the taste of wine served with the main course.

The salad that follows an important meal should be kept simple. A green salad, or a mixed salad containing tomatoes, carrots, and radishes would be appropriate. Or you could serve a single-vegetable salad using asparagus or string beans. A salad made with mixed cooked vegetables is too substantial to serve with a special meal. Instead, serve it with cheese or eggs to make a light family lunch or supper.

The abundant harvests of spring and summer, with string beans, tomatoes and asparagus bring joy and color to your salads and table. Fall and winter vegetables such as fennel and cauliflower will help you create more unusual salads.

Make sure your vegetables are thoroughly washed and dried before dressing them. To dry lettuce, place it in a kitchen cloth. Hold the corners of the cloth together and shake energetically. Then pat individual lettuce leaves dry with paper towels. Dress your salad only when ready to serve it or it will become soggy and wilted.

I am a firm believer that all good cooking begins in the market. Whether you cook Italian, Chinese or French food, the selection of first-quality ingredients will greatly determine the success of your dish. This is especially true for vegetables and salads because those ingredients will be prepared with a minimum of sauces or dressing. Very often you need not pay extra money for first-quality ingredients. You only need to recognize and select the best from what is available.

FENNEL SALAD

Insalata di Finocchi

Follow your main course with this crunchy salad

§ **MAKES 6 SERVINGS**

2 large fennel bulbs	Salt and freshly ground pepper to taste
1 tablespoon chopped parsley	3 to 4 tablespoons olive oil
1 garlic clove, finely chopped	1 tablespoon red wine vinegar

Cut off long stalks and bruised leaves from fennels. Slice ends off bulbous bases. Wash fennels thoroughly. Cut into quarters, then horizontally into thin slices. Place in a salad bowl. Add parsley and garlic. Season with salt and pepper. Add oil and vinegar; toss gently. Serve at room temperature.

CAULIFLOWER SALAD

Cavolfiore in Insalata

A great winter salad to make when lettuce is scarce and expensive.

§ **MAKES 6 SERVINGS**

1 (2- to 2½-pound) cauliflower	⅓ cup olive oil
Salt and freshly ground pepper to taste	1 to 2 tablespoons red wine vinegar

Remove leaves from cauliflower. Slice cauliflower in half. Fill a large saucepan two-thirds full with water. Bring water to a boil. Add cauliflower. Cook over high heat 15 to 20 minutes or until tender. Drain on paper towels; cool.

Detach florets from cauliflower and place in a salad bowl. Season with salt and pepper. Add oil and vinegar; toss gently. Serve at room temperature.

COOKED MIXED VEGETABLE SALAD

Insalata Cotta

A combination of fennel, beans, potatoes and carrots make a colorful addition to any meal.

MAKES 6 SERVINGS

1 large fennel bulb	2 or 3 carrots
¼ pound small string beans	1 tablespoon chopped parsley
Salt and freshly ground pepper to taste	¼ cup olive oil
2 medium potatoes	1 to 2 tablespoons red wine vinegar

Cut off long stalks and bruised leaves from fennel. Slice end off bulbous base. Wash fennel thoroughly. Cut into quarters. Fill a medium saucepan half full with salted water. Bring water to a boil. Add fennel. Cook over high heat 10 to 15 minutes or until tender but firm. Drain on paper towels; cool.

Trim and wash beans. Fill a small saucepan half full with salted water. Bring water to a boil. Add beans. Cook over high heat 5 to 10 minutes or until tender but firm. Drain on paper towels; cool.

Fill a medium saucepan two-thirds full with salted water. Bring water to a boil. Add potatoes and carrots. Cook over high heat 10 to 15 minutes. Test carrots. Remove when tender but firm. Drain on paper towels; cool. Cook potatoes 10 to 15 minutes longer or until tender but firm. Peel while hot. Cool 20 to 25 minutes.

Thinly slice fennel. Place string beans and fennel in a salad bowl. Slice carrots into ¼-inch-thick rounds. Add carrots to salad bowl. Cut potatoes into ¼-inch-thick slices. Add potatoes to salad bowl. Sprinkle vegetables with parsley. Season with salt and pepper. Add oil and vinegar; toss gently. Serve at room temperature.

TUNA AND BEAN SALAD

Insalata di Tonno e Fagioli

You will find this humble salad appetizing and surprisingly filling.

⸙ MAKES 6 SERVINGS

1½ to 2 cups dried white kidney or
    Great Northern beans
1 large red onion
2 (7-ounce) cans Italian tuna, or other
    tuna in olive oil

Salt and freshly ground pepper to taste
5 tablespoons olive oil
2 tablespoons red wine vinegar

Place beans in a large bowl. Add enough cold water to cover and let stand overnight. Drain and rinse beans thoroughly.

Place beans in a large saucepan. Add enough cold water to cover. Cover and bring to a boil. Reduce heat. Simmer 50 to 60 minutes, stirring occasionally. Drain beans and let cool.

Slice onion into thin strips. Place in a small bowl with enough cold water to cover. Let stand 1 hour, changing water several times. Drain onion. Pat dry with paper towels.

Place beans in a salad bowl. Add onion to beans. Drain oil from tuna and flake. Add to salad bowl. Season with salt and pepper. Add oil and vinegar; toss gently. Serve at room temperature.

ༀ

TOMATO SALAD

Insalata di Pomodori

Ripe tomatoes, the fragrance of basil and the goodness of olive oil capture the essence of summer.

⸙ MAKES 4 TO 6 SERVINGS

4 large tomatoes
Salt and freshly ground pepper to taste

8 to 10 fresh basil leaves
¼ cup olive oil

Wash and dry tomatoes. Cut into slices or wedges. Place tomatoes in a salad bowl. Season with salt and pepper. Tear basil leaves into pieces and add to tomatoes. Add oil; toss gently. Serve slightly chilled.

ϓ

ZUCCHINI SALAD

Zucchine in Insalata

Select zucchini that are small, firm and a shiny green.

MAKES 6 TO 8 SERVINGS

1½ **pounds zucchini**	⅓ **cup olive oil**
Juice of 2 lemons	**2 tablespoons chopped parsley**
Salt to taste	**2 garlic cloves, finely chopped**

Wash zucchini. Fill a large saucepan two-thirds full with salted water. Bring water to a boil. Add zucchini. Cook over medium heat 5 to 10 minutes, depending on size. Zucchini should be barely tender. Rinse under cold running water. Pat dry with paper towels. Slice zucchini into ¼-inch-thick rounds. Place in a salad bowl.

Combine lemon juice and salt in a small bowl. Add oil, parsley and garlic; mix until blended. Taste and adjust for seasoning. Pour dressing over zucchini. Serve slightly chilled.

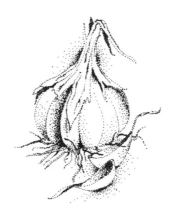

COOKED ONION SALAD

Insalata di Cipolle Cotte

The onion has been worshipped, acclaimed and vilified but our cooking would not be the same without it!

§◗ MAKES 4 TO 6 SERVINGS

5 or 6 medium yellow onions	Salt and freshly ground pepper to taste
6 tablespoons olive oil	1 to 2 tablespoons red wine vinegar

Preheat oven to 350F (175C). Cut ends off onions and peel. Fill a large saucepan half full with water. Bring water to a boil. Add onions and bring water back to a boil. Cook over high heat 2 to 3 minutes. Drain onions and rinse under cold running water. Pat dry with paper towels.

Put 2 tablespoons of the oil in a medium casserole, add onions. Bake 40 to 50 minutes or until golden. Remove from oven and cool. Slice onions. Place in a salad bowl. Season with salt and pepper. Add remaining 4 tablespoons oil and vinegar; toss gently. Serve at room temperature.

ᘔ

CABBAGE AND MUSHROOM SALAD

Insalata Appetitosa

This vitamin-packed salad is perfect for days when you don't feel like cooking.

§◗ MAKES 6 SERVINGS

½ small white cabbage	Juice of 1 lemon
½ small red cabbage	1 teaspoon mustard
½ pound small white mushrooms	Salt and freshly ground pepper to taste
¼ pound Swiss cheese	¼ cup olive oil

Remove bruised outer leaves from cabbage. Cut cabbage into thin slices. Wash and dry mushrooms thoroughly. Cut into thin slices. Cut Swiss cheese into thin strips. Place all ingredients in a salad bowl.

Combine lemon juice, mustard, salt and pepper in a small bowl. Add olive oil; mix until blended. Taste and adjust for seasoning. Pour dressing over salad; toss gently. Serve at room temperature.

༡ན

ASPARAGUS SALAD

Asparagi in Insalata

Fresh, tender asparagus is at its best with this simple oil-and-lemon dressing.

MAKES 4 TO 6 SERVINGS

2 pounds asparagus	**⅓ cup olive oil**
Juice of 1 large lemon	**2 hard-cooked eggs**
Salt to taste	

Cut off tough asparagus ends. Using a sharp knife or potato peeler, peel outer skin from asparagus. Tie asparagus together in 1 or 2 bunches with string or rubber bands.

Pour cold salted water 2 to 3 inches deep in an asparagus cooker, tall stockpot or old coffeepot. Place asparagus upright in water. Bring water to a boil. Cover and cook over high heat 6 to 8 minutes, depending on size. Remove string or rubber bands. Place 2 or 3 layers of paper towels on a large platter and place cooked asparagus on top to drain. Refrigerate until ready to serve.

A few hours before serving, remove asparagus from refrigerator. Combine lemon juice and salt in a small bowl. Add oil; mix until blended. Taste and adjust for seasoning. Remove paper towels from platter. Arrange asparagus neatly. Spoon dressing over vegetables. Remove yolks from hard-cooked eggs. Press yolks through a strainer over asparagus. Serve at room temperature.

Variation
String Bean Salad with Oil and Lemon (*Fagiolini all'Olio e Limone*): Substitute 2 pounds cooked string beans for the asparagus. Use the juice of 2 lemons and ½ cup olive oil.

MIXED SALAD

Insalata Mista

A mixed salad is almost always present at the end of an Italian meal.

⁊ MAKES 4 TO 6 SERVINGS

1 large fennel	2 medium tomatoes
2 carrots	Salt to taste
1 large red or green sweet pepper	3 to 4 tablespoons olive oil
1 small lettuce	1 tablespoon red wine vinegar

Cut off long stalks and bruised leaves from fennel. Slice end off bulbous base. Wash and dry fennel. Cut into quarters, then horizontally into thin slices. Cut carrots into thin rounds. Wash and dry pepper. Cut in half and remove pith and seeds. Cut into very thin strips.

Discard any bruised leaves from lettuce. Wash remaining leaves under cold running water. Pat dry with paper towels. Tear leaves into medium pieces. Place all vegetables in a salad bowl. Wash and dry tomatoes. Cut into slices and add to salad bowl.

When ready to serve, season with salt. Add oil and vinegar; toss gently. Serve slightly chilled.

Eggs and Sauces

An egg should have no nationality. What does one country do with an egg that another can't? After all, hard-cooked, scrambled or fried eggs can be eaten in many places around the world. Other special ways of cooking eggs are peculiar to certain countries. Americans eat eggs with bacon. The French have savory omelets. Italians have the frittata.

A frittata can be made with herbs, vegetables, cheese, fish or meat. It can also be made with jam or honey. It is said that the Romans used to mix eggs with honey. Perhaps they were the originators of the first frittata. A frittata is perfect for a light evening meal. It is excellent served cold for a snack or appetizer. In this chapter you will find four frittatas. But don't stop there; try your own variations. Don't forget about leftover meat and vegetables. They go perfectly in a frittata.

Eggs are easy to prepare and economical. They are a complete food with vitamins, sodium, protein, calcium and fat. When an egg is fresh, the yolk should be compact and the white should be transparent and tight around the yolk. Eggs are often eaten hard-cooked in a salad. They can be fried or baked with vegetables or cheese. One of my favorite ways is eggs poached in a light tomato sauce.

Think of a lovely summer day. A day you want to spend outside, gardening, swimming or reading a good book. Cooking is the last thing you want to do. But you have a family to feed—so make a frittata. Maybe the one with fresh tomatoes and basil. It will only take 10 to 15 minutes. Serve it with a green salad, crusty Italian bread and chilled white wine. Then leave the dishes and go out again, pleasantly satisfied. Enjoy the rest of your beautiful summer day.

Sauces

There are very few basic Italian sauces, but the sauces served with pasta are innumerable. These cannot be termed basic sauces because they are used only in specific dishes.

Italian cooks believe the pleasure of eating is increased by preserving the individual characteristics of ingredients. For this reason, the good Italian cook avoids the overuse of sauces. Sauces for meat, poultry and fish are usually only pan juices enriched with a little wine, broth or cream.

Basic common sense and a natural inclination toward balance guides the good Italian cook. If one course of a meal has a sauce, the chances are other courses will not. Very often sauces clash rather than complement each other. Keep this in mind when you plan a menu.

Here are a few important points to remember about Italian sauces: Use them sparingly. A sauce should enhance a dish, not overpower it. With a few exceptions, Italian sauces are best when not overcooked. Who has not been served, at one time or another, a tomato sauce so thick and dark that it tasted more like tomato paste? Overcooked sauces lose their freshness and individuality. Often Italian sauces consist simply of fresh herbs and vegetables. They are either sautéed briefly or left uncooked.

Only mayonnaise and Basic White Sauce have precise quantities and definite techniques. The remaining sauces are an extension of the cook's style. Once you understand Italian ingredients and the best way to combine their flavors, you can relax. You will gradually begin to improvise. Finally, you will learn to cook like Italians do, not with formulas but with feelings.

FRIED EGGS WITH FONTINA CHEESE

Uova Fritte con la Fontina

A light, yet filling dish that can replace meat for an impromptu supper.

MAKES 4 SERVINGS

3 to 4 tablespoons butter
8 eggs
Salt and freshly ground pepper to taste

8 slices (about ¼ pound) Italian fontina or Swiss cheese

Melt butter in a large skillet. When butter foams, break eggs into skillet. Season with salt and pepper. Cook over medium heat about 1 minute.

Place 1 slice fontina or Swiss cheese over each egg. Cover skillet and cook 6 to 8 minutes or until eggs are firm and cheese is melted. Place 2 eggs on each of 4 serving plates. Serve immediately.

EGGS WITH TOMATOES

Uova alla Diavola

This is a great low-budget meal.

MAKES 3 SERVINGS

2 cups Plain Tomato Sauce, page 208	Salt and freshly ground pepper to taste
3 tablespoons butter	6 large eggs
1 tablespoon olive oil	8 tablespoons freshly grated Parmesan
2 medium onions, thinly sliced	cheese

Prepare Plain Tomato Sauce. Melt butter with oil in a large skillet over medium heat. When butter foams, add onions. Sauté until pale yellow. Add tomato sauce and season with salt and pepper.

Break eggs into skillet and cook about 1 minute. Spoon a generous tablespoon of Parmesan cheese over each egg. Cover skillet and reduce heat. Simmer 5 to 6 minutes or until eggs are firm and cheese is melted. Place 2 eggs on each of 3 serving plates. Spoon tomato sauce around eggs. Serve immediately.

BAKED EGGS WITH PEPERONATA

Uova al Tegamino con la Peperonata

Eggs and leftover Peperonata become a light lunch or supper.

❧ **MAKES 4 SERVINGS**

1⅓ cups Peperonata, page 171	**Salt and freshly ground pepper to taste**
8 eggs	**¼ cup freshly grated Parmesan cheese**

Prepare Peperonata. Preheat oven to 350F (175C). Butter 4 ramekins.

Put ⅓ cup Peperonata in each ramekin and break 2 eggs into each one. Season with salt and pepper. Sprinkle ½ tablespoon Parmesan cheese over each egg. Bake 8 to 10 minutes or until eggs are firm and cheese is melted. Serve immediately.

Variation

Baked Eggs with Prosciutto (*Uova al Forno con Prosciutto*): Omit Peperonata. Line each ramekin with 2 or 3 slices prosciutto, page 4, or boiled ham.

ZUCCHINI FRITTATA

Frittata di Zucchine

It is important to use a heavy skillet to make a perfect frittata.

❧ **MAKES 4 SERVINGS**

6 large eggs	**1 medium onion, thinly sliced**
Salt and freshly ground pepper to taste	**3 zucchini, finely sliced**
⅓ cup freshly grated Parmesan cheese	**2 tablespoons chopped parsley**
4 tablespoons butter	**2 garlic cloves, chopped**
1 tablespoon olive oil	

Beat eggs with salt and pepper in a medium bowl. Beat in Parmesan cheese.

Melt 3 tablespoons of the butter with oil in a heavy 8- or 10-inch skillet over medium-low heat. When butter foams, add onion. Sauté about 1 minute. Add zucchini, parsley and garlic.

Sauté 3 to 4 minutes or until lightly browned. Remove zucchini mixture with a slotted spoon. Stir into egg mixture.

Melt remaining 1 tablespoon butter in skillet over medium heat. When butter foams, add egg mixture. Cook 5 to 6 minutes or until bottom of frittata is lightly browned. Place a large plate on top of skillet and turn frittata onto plate. Slide inverted frittata back into skillet. Cook 4 to 5 minutes longer. Slide frittata onto a warm serving dish. Cut into 4 wedges. Serve hot or at room temperature.

ॐ

RICOTTA CHEESE, ONION AND PARSLEY FRITTATA

Frittata di Ricotta, Cipolla e Prezzernolo

Leftover frittata makes an excellent snack or a super sandwich.

MAKES 4 SERVINGS

6 large eggs	3 tablespoons butter
Salt and freshly ground pepper to taste	1 tablespoon olive oil
1 cup ricotta cheese	1 medium onion, thinly sliced
2 tablespoons chopped parsley	

Beat eggs with salt and pepper in a medium bowl. Beat in ricotta cheese and parsley.

Melt 2 tablespoons of the butter with oil in a heavy 8- or 10-inch skillet over medium heat. When butter foams, add onion. Sauté until pale yellow. Remove onion with a slotted spoon. Stir into egg mixture.

Melt remaining 1 tablespoon butter in skillet over medium heat. When butter foams, add egg mixture. Cook 5 to 6 minutes or until bottom of frittata is lightly browned. Place a large plate on top of skillet and turn frittata onto plate. Slide inverted frittata back into skillet. Cook 4 to 5 minutes longer. Slide frittata onto a warm serving dish. Cut into 4 wedges. Serve hot or at room temperature.

Variation
Onion Frittata (*Frittata di Cipolle*): Substitute ⅓ cup freshly grated Parmesan cheese for the ricotta cheese and omit parsley. Use 2 tablespoons olive oil and 2 large onions.

TOMATO AND BASIL FRITTATA

Frittata al Pomodoro e Basilico

The variations for frittatas are endless. Only your imagination will set the limit.

℘ MAKES 4 SERVINGS

4 medium tomatoes

6 large eggs

Salt and freshly ground pepper to taste

⅓ cup freshly grated Parmesan cheese

3 tablespoons butter

1 tablespoon olive oil

2 medium onions, thinly sliced

2 garlic cloves, chopped

6 to 8 fresh basil leaves, finely chopped

Peel, seed and dice tomatoes. Beat eggs with salt and pepper in a medium bowl. Beat in Parmesan cheese.

Melt 2 tablespoons of the butter with oil in a heavy 8- or 10-inch skillet over medium heat. Add onions and garlic. Sauté until onions are pale yellow. Add tomatoes and basil. Cook 5 to 6 minutes or until tomato juices have evaporated. Remove tomato mixture with a slotted spoon. Stir into egg mixture.

Melt remaining butter in skillet over medium heat. When butter foams, add egg mixture. Cook 5 to 6 minutes or until bottom of frittata is lightly browned. Place a large plate on top of skillet and turn frittata onto plate. Slide inverted frittata back into skillet. Cook 4 to 5 minutes longer. Slide frittata onto a warm serving dish. Cut into 4 wedges. Serve hot or at room temperature.

FRIED EGGS WITH ASPARAGUS PARMA STYLE

Uova Fritte con Asparagi alla Parmigiana

Make this light treat when asparagus is plentiful.

℘ MAKES 4 SERVINGS

2½ pounds asparagus

3 tablespoons butter

8 eggs

Salt and freshly ground pepper to taste

Cut off tough asparagus ends. Using a sharp knife or potato peeler, peel outer skin from asparagus. Tie asparagus together in 1 or 2 bunches with string or rubber bands. Pour cold salted water 2 to 3 inches deep in an asparagus cooker, tall stockpot or old coffeepot. Place asparagus upright in water. Bring water to a boil. Cover and cook over high heat 6 to 8 minutes, depending on size. Drain on paper towels; remove string or rubber bands. Divide asparagus into 4 bundles. Place on 4 serving dishes.

Melt butter in a large skillet over medium heat. When butter foams, break eggs into skillet. Season with salt and pepper. Cook until firm. Place 2 eggs on top of each asparagus bundle. Serve immediately.

ᘯ

TOMATO SAUCE BOLOGNA STYLE

Salsa di Pomodoro alla Maniera di Bologna

In summer, when tomatoes are at their best, make a large quantity of this excellent sauce and freeze it.

§⊕ **MAKES 4½ CUPS**

3 pounds ripe plum tomatoes or
   overripe regular tomatoes
½ cup olive oil
2 carrots, finely chopped
2 celery stalks, finely chopped

1 medium onion, finely chopped
½ cup loosely packed fresh basil
½ cup loosely packed parsley
Salt and freshly ground pepper to taste

Cut tomatoes into large pieces. Heat oil in a large saucepan over high heat. Add tomatoes, carrots, celery, onion, basil and parsley and season with salt and pepper. Bring to a boil. Reduce heat to medium. Cook uncovered 30 to 40 minutes or until sauce reaches a medium-thick consistency. Taste and adjust for seasoning.

Press everything through a food mill and back into saucepan. Cook 20 to 30 minutes longer.

MAYONNAISE

Maionese

One of the secrets of homemade mayonnaise is to have all ingredients and utensils at room temperature.

◌ MAKES 1½ CUPS

2 egg yolks, preferably pasteurized (see Note below)	1½ cups olive oil
Salt to taste	1 tablespoon lemon juice

Place egg yolks in a round-bottom bowl. Add salt. Beat until yolks are pale yellow. Very slowly beat in a few drops of oil. Do not add oil too quickly or mayonnaise will curdle. Add remaining oil very slowly, beating constantly. Beat in lemon juice. Taste and adjust for seasoning. Refrigerate. Bring to room temperature before using.

Variations

Stir in 2 tablespoons Pesto Sauce, page 205, or 2 tablespoons Green Sauce, page 206, for green mayonnaise to serve with fish. Sauces must be at room temperature before adding to mayonnaise.

Note

Anyone with a compromised immune system, including children, the elderly or anyone with a serious illness, should not eat raw eggs because of the possibility of salmonella poisoning. If you want to make a recipe that calls for uncooked eggs, look for the pasteurized eggs that are available in some markets.

BASIC WHITE SAUCE

Salsa Balsamella

Whether French or Italian in origin, this sauce is vital to many Italian dishes.

USE THESE INGREDIENTS	TO MAKE			
	¾ cup	1½ cups	2¼ cups	3¾ cups
Milk	1 cup	2 cups	3 cups	5 cups
Butter	2 tablespoons	4 tablespoons	6 tablespoons	6 tablespoons
All-purpose flour	2 tablespoons	4 tablespoons	6 tablespoons	10 tablespoons
Salt	To taste	To taste	To taste	To taste

Bring milk almost to a boil; set aside. Melt butter in a medium saucepan. When butter foams, stir in flour. Let mixture bubble gently over low heat 1 to 2 minutes, stirring constantly. Do not let mixture brown. Whisk in milk all at once. Whisk until smooth. Season with salt. Simmer 3 to 5 minutes, whisking constantly until sauce has a medium-thick consistency. Reduce or increase cooking time for a thinner or thicker sauce. If not using immediately, rub surface of sauce with ½ tablespoon softened butter to prevent a skin from forming.

PESTO SAUCE

Pesto

If you plan to freeze the sauce, add the cheese after the sauce has thawed.

MAKES 1 CUP

3 cups loosely packed fresh basil

¾ cup olive oil

¼ cup pine nuts

3 garlic cloves, peeled

1 teaspoon salt

½ cup freshly grated Parmesan cheese

3 tablespoons Romano pecorino cheese
  or Parmesan cheese

Put basil, oil, pine nuts, garlic and salt into a blender or food processor. Process until smooth. Pour sauce into a small bowl. Add Parmesan cheese and Romano pecorino cheese or extra Parmesan cheese. Mix to blend. Taste and adjust for seasoning.

GREEN SAUCE

Salsa Verde

This sauce is the perfect accompaniment for Mixed Boiled Meats, Page 161.

≈ MAKES 3/4 CUP

1 slice white bread

2 tablespoons red wine vinegar

2 cups loosely packed parsley

2 garlic cloves, peeled

4 flat anchovy fillets

1 tablespoon capers

1/2 cup olive oil

Salt and freshly ground pepper to taste

Remove crust from bread. Tear bread into pieces and place in a small bowl. Pour vinegar over bread; let stand 10 minutes. Put into a blender or food processor. Add parsley, garlic, anchovies, capers and oil. Process until smooth. Place sauce in a small bowl. Season with salt and pepper. Refrigerate. Serve at room temperature.

Variation

Substitute lemon juice for the vinegar and serve with fish.

BOLOGNESE MEAT SAUCE

Ragù alla Bolognese

The recipe for this classic sauce has been in my family for generations.

≈ MAKES 2 1/2 TO 3 CUPS

1/4 cup butter

2 tablespoons olive oil

1 medium onion, finely chopped

1 carrot, finely chopped

1 celery stalk, finely chopped

1/4 pound pancetta, page 4, finely chopped

1 1/2 pounds ground veal

Salt and freshly ground pepper to taste

1 cup dry white wine

1 (28-ounce) can crushed Italian-style
    tomatoes

1/2 cup milk

Melt butter with oil in a large saucepan over medium heat. When butter foams, add onion, carrot, celery and pancetta. Sauté until lightly browned. Add veal. Cook, stirring, until meat is no longer pink. Season with salt and pepper. Increase heat to high and stir in wine. Cook until wine has evaporated.

Press tomatoes through a food mill or sieve to remove seeds. Stir tomato pulp into veal mixture. Cover and reduce heat. Simmer 1 to 1½ hours or until sauce reaches a medium-thick consistency; stir occasionally during cooking. Add milk and cook 5 minutes longer, stirring occasionally.

SWEET AND SOUR SAUCE

Salsa Agrodolce

A classic Bolognese sauce, this dates back to the sixteenth century.

§ **MAKES ½ CUP**

2 tablespoons tomato paste

¾ cup water

2 tablespoons butter

1 tablespoon olive oil

⅓ cup chopped parsley

4 garlic cloves, finely chopped

1 teaspoon all-purpose flour

1 tablespoon sugar

2 tablespoons red wine vinegar

Salt and freshly ground pepper to taste

Mix tomato paste and water in a small bowl. Melt butter with oil in a small saucepan over low heat. When butter foams, add parsley and garlic. Sauté until garlic begins to color. Stir in flour and sugar. Stir in vinegar and diluted tomato paste; mix until blended. Season with salt and pepper. Cook over medium heat 4 to 5 minutes, stirring frequently.

PLAIN TOMATO SAUCE

Salsa di Pomodoro Semplice

Many recipes in this book will need some of this sauce.

§ **MAKES ABOUT 2 CUPS**

1 tablespoon olive oil

1 (28-oz.) can crushed Italian-style tomatoes

Salt and freshly ground pepper to taste

Heat oil in a medium saucepan over medium heat. Press tomatoes through a food mill or sieve to remove seeds. Add tomato pulp to saucepan. Simmer uncovered 15 to 20 minutes. Season with salt and pepper.

Desserts

*T*here is no doubt most Italians would rather miss dessert than a first course. After all, at the end of an Italian meal you don't have room for a rich dessert. Fresh fruit, on the other hand, will refresh the palate and end the meal on a pleasant, light note.

For centuries, Italy has produced some of the best desserts in Europe. Anyone who has walked through Italian cities and looked at pastry shops will agree. Rich and elaborate desserts are generally store-bought and served on special occasions. On Sundays, many families go to pastry shops to buy *paste miste*, assorted pastries to complete the Sunday meal.

Italy also has an incredible number of less complicated desserts called *dolci casalinghi*, family cakes. These are usually items like jam or fruit tarts or fruit cakes. They are simple to make and do not involve difficult techniques. Most keep well for several days and are not overly sweet. When an unexpected guest arrives, a slice of moist apple cake or crisp walnut pie is served with the ritual cup of espresso coffee.

Many families have their own version of a particular cake. The recipe is handed down from generation to generation and the cake is considered a showpiece. Generally this cake is prepared for a family celebration or a religious holiday.

Because elaborate desserts do not play an important role in Italian home cooking, most desserts in this chapter are easy to make. A few require a little more skill and patience.

In 1960, I arrived in the United States as the young bride of an American doctor. I was suddenly faced with desserts served at the end of almost every meal. In spite of the rich Bolognese cuisine, I never had had a weight problem. So I enthusiastically explored these new, rich and creamy desserts. Of all the desserts, my favorite was American apple pie. I had apple pie every day, sometimes twice a day, sometimes with ice cream on top. And slowly I began to grow—sideways. I finally realized that all my clothes were too small and decided to weigh myself. I was 20 pounds overweight. Apple pie did what pasta couldn't.

It is important to know what kind of dessert to serve on specific occasions. For a formal, elegant dinner choose an impressive dessert. In doing so, keep in mind the dinner that precedes it. Decide on a dessert that will complement it.

You should also keep in mind the season. In spring and summer, lighter desserts are preferable, such as Strawberry Mousse or Maria Angela's Meringue Cake. Fall and winter allow you to indulge in richer desserts like Italian Rum Cake or Chocolate Mousse. For an informal get-together you will never go wrong with Sweet Pasta Fritters. Pile them on an attractive plate so adults and children can serve themselves.

Let's not forget fresh fruit. It should always be present in an Italian dinner. In winter, slice oranges and serve them with a liqueur sauce—or poach some ripe pears in red wine. In summer, choose the best strawberries, raspberries, peaches and apricots. Arrange them beautifully on a large platter and you will have an eye-catching instant dessert.

APPLE FRITTERS

Frittelle di Mele

Most countries have an apple fritter dessert. This is the Northern Italian version.

§ꙮ **MAKES 4 TO 6 SERVINGS**

4 large apples

¾ cup plus ⅓ cup sugar

5 tablespoons rum or other liquor

2 eggs, separated, at room temperature

¾ cup milk

6 tablespoons all-purpose flour

Pinch of salt

Oil for frying

⅓ cup sugar

Core and peel apples and cut into rounds. Combine apples, 3¼ cup sugar and rum or other liquor in a large bowl. Cover bowl and let apples marinate 2 to 3 hours.

Beat egg yolks in a medium bowl. Beat in milk. Gradually sift in flour, mixing constantly. Beat egg whites and salt in a small bowl until stiff. Fold beaten whites into batter.

Pour oil 2 inches deep in a large saucepan or deep-fryer. Heat oil to 375F (190C) or until a 1-inch cube of bread turns golden brown almost immediately. Dip apple rounds into batter. Using a slotted spoon, lower a few rounds at a time into hot oil. Turn fritters. When golden on both sides, remove from oil with slotted spoon. Drain on paper towels.

Arrange drained fritters on a platter. Sprinkle with ⅓ cup sugar. Serve hot.

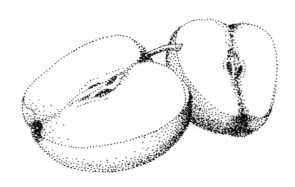

RICE FRITTERS

Frittelle di Riso

You will eat these fritters as fast as you can make them.

§ **MAKES 6 TO 8 SERVINGS**

2 cups milk

½ cup arborio rice, page 5, or other
   short-grain rice

2 tablespoons butter

½ cup granulated sugar

Grated zest of 1 lemon

3 eggs, separated, at room temperature

6 tablespoons all-purpose flour

3 tablespoons rum

Pinch of salt

Oil for frying

Powdered sugar

Bring milk to a boil in a medium saucepan. Add rice and cook uncovered over medium heat 10 minutes. Stir in butter, granulated sugar and lemon zest. Cook 15 to 20 minutes longer, stirring mixture several times. When rice is done, all milk should be absorbed.

Place rice mixture in a bowl to cool until it is just warm. When rice is warm, add egg yolks, flour and rum; mix well. Beat egg whites and salt in a medium bowl until stiff. Fold beaten whites into rice mixture.

Pour oil 2 inches deep in a large saucepan or deep-fryer. Heat oil to 375F (190C) or until a 1-inch cube of bread turns golden brown almost immediately. Drop batter a few tablespoon-fuls at a time into hot oil. Turn fritters. When golden on both sides, remove from oil with a slotted spoon. Drain on paper towels.

Arrange drained fritters on a platter. Sprinkle with powdered sugar. Serve hot.

CHEESE FRITTERS

Frittelle di Ricotta

Watch these Cheese Fritters puff up into little golden balls.

MAKES 8 SERVINGS

4 eggs	1 pound ricotta cheese
½ cup granulated sugar	1 cup all-purpose flour
Few drops of vanilla extract	Oil for frying
2 teaspoons baking powder	Powdered sugar

In a large bowl, beat eggs until fluffy. Add granulated sugar, vanilla and baking powder; mix well. Mix in ricotta cheese. Fold in flour a little at a time. Cover bowl and let batter stand at room temperature 1 hour.

Pour oil 2 inches deep in a large saucepan or deep-fryer. Heat oil to 375F (190C) or until a 1-inch cube of bread turns golden brown almost immediately. Drop batter a few tablespoonfuls at a time into hot oil. Turn fritters. When golden on both sides, remove from oil with a slotted spoon. Drain on paper towels.

Arrange drained fritters on a platter. Sprinkle with powdered sugar. Serve hot.

SWEET PASTA FRITTERS

Sfrappole

Eat *Sfrappole* in Bologna and *Cenci* in Florence. Each region has a different name for this dessert.

⁊ MAKES 10 TO 12 SERVINGS

2 cups all-purpose flour

2 eggs

¼ cup butter, very soft for hand mixing, or cold and in small pieces for food processor

⅓ cup granulated sugar

3 tablespoons rum

3 to 4 tablespoons chilled sweet white wine

Oil for frying

Powdered sugar or honey

To make by hand: Place flour on a wooden board and make a well in the center. Break eggs into well and beat lightly with a fork. Add butter, granulated sugar, rum and wine. Mix thoroughly with eggs. Using your hands, gradually add flour starting from inside of well and work into a ball.

To make using a food processor: Place flour, eggs, butter, sugar and rum in processor with a metal blade. Process until ingredients are blended. Add wine and process until dough forms a ball.

Wrap dough in waxed paper and refrigerate 20 to 25 minutes. Roll out dough ⅛ inch thick. Using a pastry wheel or a sharp knife, cut dough into strips ¾ inch wide and 6 or 7 inches long. Tie strips into bows.

Pour oil 2 inches deep in a large saucepan or deep-fryer. Heat oil to 375F (190C) or until a 1-inch cube of bread turns golden brown almost immediately. Using a slotted spoon, lower pasta bows a few at a time into hot oil. Turn bows. When golden brown on both sides, remove from oil with slotted spoon. Drain on paper towels.

Arrange drained bows on a platter and dust generously with powdered sugar, or drizzle with honey. Serve at room temperature.

BAKED APPLES WITH CUSTARD CREAM

Mele Cotte alla Crema Pasticcera

The combination of piping hot apples and custard makes this an ideal winter dessert.

MAKES 8 SERVINGS

8 large Golden Delicious apples	Few drops of vanilla extract
4 tablespoons butter	6 egg yolks
½ cup Marsala wine or sherry	6 tablespoons sugar
½ cup sugar	¼ cup all-purpose flour
Custard Cream	
2 cups milk	

Preheat oven to 350F (175C). Butter a large shallow baking dish. Core apples. Fill each apple with ½ tablespoon butter, 1 tablespoon Marsala or sherry and 1 tablespoon sugar. Place apples in buttered baking dish. Bake 40 to 50 minutes or until apple skins begin to split.

While apples are baking prepare Custard Cream: Bring milk to a boil with vanilla in a medium saucepan. In a large heavy saucepan off the heat, beat egg yolks and sugar until pale and thick. Beat in flour until well blended. Very slowly pour in hot milk, beating constantly. Cook custard cream over medium heat 5 to 8 minutes, beating constantly. Do not boil. Custard cream is done when it coats the back of a spoon.

Place baked apples on a serving dish. Spoon hot custard cream over each apple. Serve hot or at room temperature.

BAKED APPLE, PEAR, DATE AND WALNUT ROLL

Rotolo di Frutta

This lovely dessert is a variation of the classic apple strudel, a typical dessert of the Trentino-Alto Adige region.

MAKES 10 TO 12 SERVINGS

Sweet Pie Pastry, page 218

2 large Golden Delicious apples, peeled
 and thinly sliced

2 large Bosc pears, peeled and thinly
 sliced

8 ounces dates, finely chopped

5 ounces walnuts, finely chopped

2 ounces blanched almonds, finely
 chopped

Grated zest of 1 lemon

¼ cup rum

1 cup strawberry or plum jam

4 Amaretti di Saronno cookies, crushed

1 large egg, lightly beaten

Powdered sugar

Prepare Sweet Pie Pastry. Preheat oven to 375F (165C). Butter a 15 × 12-inch baking sheet.

In a large bowl, combine apples, pears, dates, walnuts and almonds. On a lightly floured surface, roll out the dough very thinly. With a scalloped pastry wheel, cut the dough into a rectangle, about 20 inches long and 10 inches wide. Roll the dough quite loosely over the rolling pin and lift. Place a large kitchen towel under the pastry dough, then unroll the dough over the towel. Spread the crumbled Amaretti cookies over the pastry dough, leaving a 2-inch border on 3 sides, and a 4-inch border on the side nearest you.

Spread the apple filling evenly over the cookie crumbs. Fold the 4-inch border over the filling, then pick up the edges of the towel near you, and roll the pastry over loosely, away from you. When the pastry is all rolled up, pinch the sides of the pastry to seal.

Pick up the edges of the towel and gently slide the roll onto the buttered baking sheet, with the seam facing up. Brush the top and sides of the roll with the beaten egg and bake 50 to 60 minutes, or until dough is golden brown. Remove from the oven and cool to room temperature. Dust with powdered sugar and serve.

BAKED STUFFED PEACHES

Pesche Ripiene al Forno

Amaretto di Saronno cookies are found in Italian specialty stores.

MAKES 6 SERVINGS

6 firm ripe peaches
½ cup sugar
½ cup sliced blanched almonds
6 large Amaretto di Saronno cookies or
   almond macaroons, broken

1 egg yolk
⅓ cup Amaretto di Saronno liqueur or
   other liqueur

Preheat oven to 350F (175C). Butter a large shallow baking dish. Wash and dry peaches and cut into halves. Remove pits and scoop out not more than 1 tablespoon pulp from each half.

In a blender or food processor fitted with a metal blade, combine peach pulp, sugar, almonds, cookies, egg yolk and liqueur. Blend to a fine paste. Divide mixture between peach halves. Arrange peaches in a single layer in buttered baking dish. Bake 20 to 25 minutes. Serve warm or at room temperature.

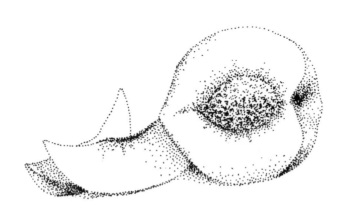

PEARS POACHED IN RED WINE

Pere al Vino Rosso

In Italy, wine and fruit are often combined into desserts like this one.

✦ MAKES 8 SERVINGS

8 firm ripe pears, preferably Bosc	¾ cup sugar
4 cups good dry red wine	Grated zest of 1 lemon
1 cup Marsala wine or sherry	Juice of 1 lemon

Peel pears leaving stems attached. Flatten the pear bottoms by cutting off a thin slice from each. Stand pears close together in a large saucepan or casserole. Add red wine, Marsala or sherry, ½ cup sugar and lemon zest. Bring to a boil. Reduce heat to medium and cover pan. Cook pears 25 to 30 minutes or until tender, basting several times during cooking.

Place pears in a glass bowl or platter. Let stand at room temperature until ready to serve. Add ¼ cup sugar and lemon juice to liquid in pan. Boil until it has the consistency of syrup, 15 to 20 minutes. Spoon hot sauce over pears and serve.

✄

JAM TART

Crostata di Marmellata

White wine adds a subtle flavor to this pastry.

✦ MAKES 10 SERVINGS

Sweet Pie Pastry	2 tablespoons sugar
2 cups all-purpose flour	3 to 4 tablespoons chilled white wine
⅔ cup butter, at room temperature for hand mixing, or cold and in small pieces for food processor	1 (12-ounce) jar strawberry or other jam
1 egg	1 egg, lightly beaten

Prepare Sweet Pie Pastry: In a medium bowl using a pastry blender or in a food processor fitted with a metal blade, mix flour and butter until crumbly. Add egg, sugar and wine; mix until dough is completely moistened. Place dough on a flat surface and work into a ball. Wrap in waxed paper and refrigerate at least 1 hour.

Butter a 10-inch tart pan with a removable bottom. Preheat oven to 375F (190C). Reserve one-third of pastry dough for lattice decoration.

On a lightly floured surface, roll out remaining dough to a 12-inch circle. Carefully place dough in buttered tart pan. Trim edges of dough by gently pressing the rolling pin over top of pan. Prick bottom of pastry shell several times with a fork.

Spread jam in pastry shell. Roll out reserved dough ⅛ inch thick. Using a pastry cutter or sharp knife, cut dough into ¾-inch strips. Lay strips across tart to make a lattice, joining strips where necessary. Brush dough with beaten egg.

Bake 30 to 40 minutes or until crust is golden brown. Let stand at least 30 minutes before removing from pan. Cut into thin slices.

ༀ

ALMOND CAKE

Torta di Mandorle

This cake will keep several days without refrigeration.

§ MAKES 10 SERVINGS

1 pkg. active dry yeast	Grated zest of 1 lemon
⅓ cup warm water (110F, 43C)	¾ cup granulated sugar
1 cup blanched almonds	1½ cups self-rising flour
3 eggs, lightly beaten	Powdered sugar
½ cup butter, at room temperature	

Preheat oven to 350F (175C). Butter an 8-inch-round cake pan with a removable bottom. Stir yeast into warm water until dissolved.

Chop almonds into very small pieces. In a large bowl or food processor fitted with the metal blade, combine eggs, butter, lemon zest, granulated sugar, flour, yeast mixture and almonds. Mix thoroughly.

Pour batter into buttered pan. Bake 30 to 40 minutes or until cake is golden. Cool in pan 30 minutes. Place cake on a platter and dust with powdered sugar. Serve at room temperature.

STRAWBERRY MOUSSE

Spuma di Fragole

Cool and pretty, this is a perfect dessert for a summer dinner party.

☙ MAKES 10 SERVINGS

8 cups strawberries (about 4 baskets)	½ cup hot water
¾ cup sugar	1½ cups whipping cream
½ cup Marsala wine or ⅓ cup liqueur	Additional strawberries
Juice of 1 lemon	Whipped cream
3 envelopes unflavored gelatin	

Wash and hull strawberries. In a blender or food processor fitted with a metal blade, puree strawberries and sugar. Place strawberry mixture in a large bowl and stir in Marsala or liquor and lemon juice.

Stir gelatin into hot water until dissolved. Stir into strawberry mixture. Whip cream to medium thickness; fold into strawberry mixture.

Pour mousse into a large glass bowl or spoon into individual glasses. Refrigerate overnight. Before serving, decorate with additional strawberries and whipped cream. Serve chilled.

CHOCOLATE MOUSSE

Spuma di Cioccolata

For an excitingly different taste, add three or four tablespoons of orange-flavored liqueur or rum.

❧ MAKES 6 SERVINGS

8 ounces semisweet chocolate, cut into small pieces

3 eggs, preferably pasteurized (see Note, page 204)

1 cup whipping cream

Whipped cream

Grated chocolate

Preheat oven to 200F (95C). Put chocolate pieces into a small ovenproof bowl and place in oven until chocolate has melted, 4 to 5 minutes. Remove chocolate from oven and set aside to cool slightly.

Beat eggs until foamy in a medium bowl. Beat 1 cup cream until stiff in a large bowl. Add eggs, a little at a time to cooled chocolate, beating at low speed. Do not overbeat. Fold chocolate mixture thoroughly into whipped cream.

Spoon mousse into a large glass bowl or into individual glasses. Decorate with additional whipped cream and grated chocolate. Refrigerate overnight. Serve chilled.

ZABAGLIONE-MASCARPONE RASPBERRY TRIFLE

Zuppa di Zabaglione e Mascarpone

This mouthwatering, luscious dessert is simple to prepare. Do not attempt to make it without mascarpone and imported Amaretti di Saronno cookies.

✑ MAKES 8 SERVINGS

8 eggs, separated	Juice of 1 lemon
1⅓ cups sugar	½ cup dark rum
½ cup sweet Marsala wine or sherry	1½ cups water
1¼ pounds mascarpone cheese	32 pairs Italian Amaretti di Saronno
⅓ cup water	cookies
Pinch of cream of tartar	Fresh berries or chocolate shavings
2 cups fresh or thawed frozen raspberries	

In a large bowl or top part of a double boiler, beat egg yolks and ¼ cup of the sugar until pale yellow. Set over simmering water. Add Marsala or sherry, beating well after each addition. Cook and beat until thickened and hot to the touch. Transfer to a bowl and cool.

Place mascarpone into a medium bowl and fold in cooled zabaglione, a bit at a time, until everything is well blended.

In a small skillet combine ½ cup of the sugar and the ⅓ cup water and bring to a boil over medium heat. Stir once or twice. Cook until the syrup thickens and turns lightly golden and is at the soft ball stage, about 2 minutes.

While the syrup is cooking, put the egg whites, ¼ cup of the sugar and the cream of tartar in bowl of an electric mixer and beat on high speed until stiff peaks form. Reduce speed to medium and pour syrup slowly into egg whites. (Do not pour it directly over the beater.) Fold beaten egg whites into zabaglione-mascarpone mixture and set aside.

Drain frozen raspberries, if using. In a blender or food processor fitted with the metal blade, combine raspberries, remaining ⅓ cup sugar and the lemon juice and process into a thick sauce. Press sauce through a sieve into a bowl to remove seeds.

In a medium bowl combine rum and water. Place cookies in a large, shallow baking pan and pour rum mixture over them. After 2 minutes, turn cookies over to soak on the other side. Soak 2 to 3 minutes. Place 3 cookies in each of 8 individual dessert glasses and top them with some mascarpone mixture. Spoon raspberry sauce over the mascarpone mixture. Cover sauce with 4 to 5 cookies each and top with another layer of mascarpone mixture. Cover glasses with plastic wrap and refrigerate several hours or overnight. Before serving, decorate each glass with some fresh berries or chocolate shavings.

ॡ

FAMILY-STYLE APPLE CAKE

Torta di Mele alla Casalinga

A splendid cake for any occasion, pears can be used instead of apples.

§ዐ **MAKES 8 TO 10 SERVINGS**

1 package active dry yeast	**½ cup butter, at room temperature**
⅓ cup warm water (110F, 43C)	**2 cups self-rising flour**
3 eggs	**4 large apples, cored, peeled, thinly sliced**
½ cup plus 1 to 2 tablespoons sugar	

Preheat oven to 375F (190C). Butter and flour a 10-inch-round cake pan with a removable bottom. Stir yeast into warm water until dissolved.

Beat eggs and ½ cup sugar in a large bowl until pale and thick. Beat in butter, flour and yeast mixture. Add three-quarters of the apples to batter; mix with a spatula.

Pour batter into buttered pan. Arrange remaining apple slices over batter. Sprinkle 1 to 2 tablespoons sugar over batter. Bake 35 to 45 minutes or until cake is golden. Cool to room temperature, then remove cake from pan. This cake keeps well in the refrigerator for several days. Return to room temperature before serving.

RICE CAKE

Torta di Riso

Rice cake is a specialty of Bologna, and from Bologna with love, I want to share this cake with you.

MAKES 6 TO 8 SERVINGS

4½ cups milk	5 eggs
1½ cups sugar	½ cup blanched almonds, finely chopped
Grated zest of 1 lemon	½ cup candied citron, finely chopped
¾ cup arborio rice, page 5, or other short-grain rice	¼ cup plus 2 to 3 tablespoons rum
	Whipped cream

Preheat oven to 350F (175C). Butter a 10-inch-round cake pan with a removable bottom. Sprinkle pan with fine unflavored bread crumbs and shake off excess crumbs.

Combine milk, sugar and lemon zest in a medium saucepan; bring to a boil. Stir in rice and reduce heat. Simmer uncovered 45 minutes to 1 hour or until all the liquid is absorbed. Remove from heat and let cool.

Beat eggs until foamy in a large bowl. Add cooled rice mixture, almonds, candied citron and ¼ cup rum. Mix thoroughly.

Pour rice mixture into buttered pan and level top with a spatula. Bake 40 to 45 minutes or until a wooden pick inserted in center of cake comes out dry. Pierce holes in top of cake with a fork and sprinkle with 2 to 3 tablespoons rum. Cool to room temperature before removing cake from pan. Decorate with whipped cream.

SWEET SPINACH AND CHEESE CAKE

Erbazzone Dolce all'Emiliana

Omit the sugars and liqueur and you will have a perfect luncheon dish.

MAKES 10 SERVINGS

Sweet Pie Pastry, page 218
1½ (10-ounce) pkgs. frozen spinach
1½ cups blanched almonds
1 cup plus 1 tablespoon granulated sugar
1 pound ricotta cheese

4 eggs, separated, at room temperature
⅓ cup almond liqueur or other liqueur
Pinch of salt
Powdered sugar

Prepare Sweet Pie Pastry. Preheat oven to 375F (190C). Butter a 10-inch-round cake pan with a removable bottom.

Cook spinach according to package instructions. Squeeze spinach to remove as much moisture as possible. Finely chop spinach with a knife or in a food processor fitted with a metal blade; do not puree.

Finely chop almonds. In a large bowl, combine almonds, spinach, 1 cup granulated sugar, ricotta cheese, egg yolks and liqueur; mix well. Beat egg whites, salt and 1 tablespoon granulated sugar in a medium bowl until stiff. Fold beaten whites into spinach mixture.

On a lightly floured surface, roll out dough to a 13-inch circle. Place dough carefully in buttered cake pan. Pour spinach mixture into pastry shell and level the filling with a spatula. Bake 1 hour or until top of cake is golden. Cool cake in pan. Place cool cake on a platter. Sprinkle top with powdered sugar. Serve at room temperature.

FRIED FRUIT

Fritto Misto di Frutta

Fresh fruit as you have never tasted it, it's coated with a light batter and fried.

MAKES 6 TO 8 SERVINGS

2 eggs, separated, at room temperature	20 to 25 strawberries
2 tablespoons plus 1 teaspoon sugar	2 apples
1 tablespoon olive oil	2 pears
2 tablespoons brandy or rum	4 bananas
1 cup beer	Oil for frying
1½ cups all-purpose flour	Sugar
Pinch of salt	

Beat egg yolks, 2 tablespoons sugar, olive oil and brandy or rum in a large bowl. Add beer and beat until blended. Gradually sift in flour, beating until batter is smooth and has the consistency of thick sour cream. Cover bowl and let batter stand at room temperature 2 to 3 hours.

Beat egg whites, salt and 1 teaspoon sugar in a medium bowl until stiff. Fold beaten whites into batter.

Wash and hull strawberries; dry with paper towels. Core and peel apples and pears. Peel bananas. Cut apples, pears and bananas into ½-inch pieces.

Pour oil 2 inches deep in a large saucepan or deep-fryer. Heat oil to 375F (190C) or until a 1-inch cube of bread turns golden brown almost immediately. Dip pieces of fruit into batter. Using a slotted spoon, lower fruit a few pieces at a time into hot oil. When fruit is golden all over, remove from oil with slotted spoon. Drain on paper towels.

Arrange drained fruit on a platter and sprinkle with sugar. Serve hot.

WALNUT AND HONEY PIE

La Bonissima

A pie from Modena, it's named after a medieval noblewoman who sold all her jewelry to help the poor.

§● **MAKES 8 TO 10 SERVINGS**

Sweet Pie Pastry, page 218
2½ cups chopped walnuts
¾ cup honey

⅓ cup rum
1 egg, lightly beaten

Prepare Sweet Pie Pastry. Divide dough into 2 balls. Wrap each in waxed paper and refrigerate at least 1 hour. On a lightly floured surface, roll out 1 ball of dough to a 12-inch circle. Carefully place dough in a 10-inch-round tart pan with a removable bottom. Prick bottom of pastry shell with a fork. Refrigerate pastry shell until ready to use.

Preheat oven to 375F (190C). Place walnuts in a medium bowl. Add honey and rum; mix to blend. Spread walnut mixture evenly in pastry shell.

Roll out remaining ball of dough to a 10-inch circle. Place carefully over walnut filling. Pinch edges of top dough with bottom dough to seal. Brush surface with beaten egg. Prick top of pie in 5 or 6 places with a fork.

Bake 40 minutes or until crust is golden. Let stand at least 15 minutes before removing from pan and serving.

SWEET TORTELLI EMILIA-ROMAGNA STYLE

Tortelli Dolci all'Emiliana

Yummy is the word to describe these sweet tortelli—another family-style dessert and another winner.

§ᴥ **MAKES 8 TO 10 SERVINGS**

2½ cups all-purpose flour

3 eggs

⅓ cup granulated sugar

Grated zest of 1 lemon

½ cup butter, very soft for hand mixing, or cold and in small pieces for food processor

⅓ cup chilled white wine

Strawberry or other jam

Oil for frying

Powdered sugar

To make by hand: Place flour on a pastry board and make a well in the center. Break eggs into well and beat lightly with a fork. Add granulated sugar, lemon zest, butter and wine. Mix thoroughly with eggs. Using your hands, gradually add flour starting from inside of well and work into a ball.

To make using a food processor: Place flour, eggs, sugar, lemon zest and butter in food processor with a metal blade. Process until ingredients are blended. Add wine and process until dough forms a ball.

Wrap dough in waxed paper and refrigerate 1 hour. On a lightly floured surface, roll out dough ⅛ inch thick. Using a 3-inch round scalloped pastry cutter or a glass, cut dough into circles. Put 1 heaping teaspoon jam into each circle of dough. Fold each circle in half and press edges firmly.

Pour oil 2 inches deep in a large saucepan or deep-fryer. Heat oil to 375F (190C) or until a 1-inch cube of bread turns golden brown almost immediately. Using a slotted spoon, lower tortelli a few at a time into hot oil. Turn tortelli. When golden brown on both sides, remove from oil with slotted spoon. Drain on paper towels.

Arrange drained tortelli on a platter and sprinkle with powdered sugar. Serve hot.

HOT ZABAGLIONE

Zabaglione Caldo

A classic Italian dessert that needs no introduction.

MAKES 6 TO 8 SERVINGS

8 egg yolks
½ cup sugar
¾ cup dry Marsala wine, sherry or port

In a large bowl or the top part of a double boiler, beat egg yolks and sugar until pale and thick. Set bowl or top part of double boiler over simmering water; do not let water boil. Add Marsala, sherry or port slowly, beating constantly. Zabaglione is ready when mixture has tripled in volume and it is soft and fluffy, 4 to 6 minutes. Spoon into individual glasses. Serve immediately.

Variation

Cold Zabaglione (*Zabaglione Freddo*): As soon as Zabaglione swells up into a soft mass, set bowl or top part of a double boiler over a bowl of ice water. Continue stirring until cool. Spoon into glasses and refrigerate until ready to serve.

SWEET FRIED CREAM

Crema Fritta

Transform staple ingredients into this delicate and delicious dessert.

2 cups milk

6 egg yolks

6 tablespoons granulated sugar

Grated zest of 1 lemon

¼ cup all-purpose flour

1½ cups very fine, dry unflavored bread
  crumbs

2 eggs, lightly beaten

Oil for frying

⅓ cup powdered sugar

Bring milk to a boil in a medium saucepan. In a large heavy saucepan off the heat, beat egg yolks, granulated sugar and lemon zest until pale and thick. Beat in flour until well blended. Very slowly pour in hot milk, beating constantly. Cook custard cream over medium heat 5 to 8 minutes, beating constantly. Do not let boil. Custard cream is done when it coats the back of a spoon.

Moisten a large plate or cookie sheet with water. Spread cooked cream to a thickness of ½ to 1 inch. Cream can be prepared to this point a day or two ahead and refrigerated. When cream is completely cooled, cut into squares or diamonds.

Place bread crumbs in a shallow dish. Coat cream shapes with bread crumbs. Dip coated cream shapes into beaten eggs, and coat again with bread crumbs.

Pour oil 2 inches deep in a large saucepan or deep-fryer. Heat oil to 375F (190C) or until a 1-inch cube of bread turns golden brown almost immediately. Using a slotted spoon, lower cream pieces a few at a time into hot oil. Turn cream pieces. When golden on both sides, remove from oil with slotted spoon. Drain on paper towels.

Arrange drained fried cream on a platter and sprinkle with powdered sugar. Serve hot.

MOCHA GELATO

Gelato di Caffé

The coffee enhances the chocolate flavor of this luscious treat.

§● MAKES 6 TO 8 SERVINGS

3 cups milk

1 vanilla bean

6 egg yolks

¾ cup sugar

1 cup whipping cream

2 tablespoons instant espresso powder or
regular instant coffee

4 ounces semisweet chocolate, cut into
small pieces

Prepare a custard: Heat milk with vanilla bean in a medium saucepan over medium heat. In a medium bowl, beat egg yolks and sugar until pale yellow and soft ribbons are formed. Add the hot milk to the eggs, very slowly, beating after each addition. Transfer the mixture back into the saucepan and place over medium-low heat. Beat constantly without letting the milk boil, cooking the custard 2 to 3 minutes. (The custard is done when it evenly coats the back of a spoon.) Discard the vanilla bean, strain the custard into a clean bowl and cool to room temperature. (The custard can be prepared up to this point and kept tightly covered in the refrigerator up to 2 days.)

Combine the cream with the coffee in a small saucepan. Heat the cream to a simmer over medium heat, mixing with a wire whisk. Remove from heat. Add chocolate and mix until it is melted. Cool, then add to custard. Freeze in an ice-cream maker according to manufacturer's instructions.

EGG CUSTARD AND CHOCOLATE SWIRL GELATO

Stracciatella

Italian gelato is lighter than American ice cream. It has a denser, softer texture and a fresh, not-too-sweet taste. Gelato is also considerably lower in butterfat because more milk is used than cream. Ideally gelato should be served immediately or within a few hours after it is made. Freezing changes the texture of gelato.

§ **MAKES ABOUT 1 QUART**

1 recipe Egg Custard Gelato, page 235
4 ounces good-quality bittersweet
   chocolate, coarsely chopped

1 tablespoon crème de cacao, or other
   liqueur of your choice
⅓ cup heavy cream

Prepare egg custard and chill in refrigerator about 1 hour. Place in bowl of ice-cream machine and freeze it according to manufacturer's instructions.

Meanwhile, put 1 or 2 inches of water in a small saucepan and bring to a boil. Put chocolate, crème de cacao and cream in a medium metal bowl and set it over pan. Turn heat off. Stir occasionally until chocolate is completely melted. Cool chocolate to room temperature.

When gelato is completely frozen, scoop it up and place into a large chilled bowl. Slowly, dribble in some of cooled chocolate and, with the sharp edge of a spatula, using a crisscross motion, roughly mix it with gelato to create swirls.

Serve gelato immediately, or transfer it to an airtight container and freeze it 1 or 2 days.

WARM BERRIES IN
VODKA SAUCE WITH CUSTARD GELATO

Frutti di Bosco alla Vodka e Gelato di Crema

At the end of a multi-course meal at Franco Rossi in Bologna, Franco, the owner of the restaurant, brought to table a large *coppa* of egg custard gelato topped by vividly bright mixed berries that had been tossed in caramelized sugar and vodka. It was a simple, yet magnificent end to a very good summer meal.

℘ MAKES 4 SERVINGS

1 recipe Egg Custard Gelato, page 235
2 cups mixed berries of your choice, washed and patted dry with paper towels

¼ cup water
⅓ cup sugar
¼ cup vodka

Prepare egg custard and chill in refrigerator about 1 hour. Place in bowl of ice-cream machine and freeze it according to manufacturer's instructions. Transfer to a freezer for a few hours. About 15 minutes before you plan to serve it, transfer gelato to refrigerator.

If using strawberries, hull them and cut into quarters. Put the water and sugar in a large skillet over medium heat, and stir until sugar is completely dissolved and has a nice glossy, thick, brown color. Remove skillet from heat and add vodka. Place skillet back on medium heat and stir until sauce has a thick caramel texture. Add berries and stir just long enough to heat berries through and to coat them with caramelized sauce, 1 to 2 minutes.

Spoon gelato into chilled serving glasses, top with some of mixed berries and their juices, and serve at once.

Tip

Cooking with alcohol: When cooking with wine or liquor, make sure that the pan is away from any flames and off the burner before adding alcohol. Otherwise, the flame may ignite the alcohol in the bottle and cause it to explode while you are pouring it. Always be cautious when cooking with alcohol.

ESPRESSO-CARAMEL CUSTARD

Fior di Latte al Caffé

When properly prepared, *fior di latte*, one of the most popular desserts served in the trattorie of Italy, is absolutely outstanding. A good *fior di latte* should have a creamy consistency and a firm texture. It should be free of unappealing bubbles, and it should ooze and shine with the coating of caramel syrup.

MAKES 6 SERVINGS

Caramel Syrup
½ cup sugar
¼ cup water

Espresso-Caramel Custard
2 cups milk

1 cup brewed Italian espresso or strong American coffee
6 large eggs
⅓ cup sugar

Prepare syrup: Combine sugar and water in a small saucepan. Cook over high heat until mixture is thick and bubbling and has a rich golden brown color, 5 to 6 minutes.

Pour caramel quickly into 6 small custard molds, tilting and rotating molds to coat bottom evenly. Set aside until sugar has hardened completely, 8 to 10 minutes. (To clean hard syrup from pan, fill it with water, bring it to a boil and scrape sugar off.)

Preheat oven to 350F (175C).

Prepare custard: In a medium saucepan, bring milk and espresso to a gentle boil. Reduce heat to low and simmer uncovered making sure that milk does not cook over, until mixture is reduced to about three-quarters of its original amount, about 20 minutes. Remove pan from heat.

In a medium bowl, beat eggs and sugar until well combined. Very slowly add eggs to milk mixture, mixing constantly with a wire whisk. Strain mixture into a clean bowl and pour into prepared molds. Place molds in a large baking pan and add enough water in pan to come halfway up sides of molds. Cover with aluminum foil and place pan on middle rack of oven.

Bake 20 minutes, then turn pan around and bake 15 minutes more. Turn pan around one more time and bake 5 to 10 minutes more. Test doneness of custard by tapping side of mold. If custard wiggles, cook 5 minutes longer. Cool custard. (Custard can be prepared several hours or a day ahead. Refrigerate tightly covered.)

To serve, run a thin knife around rim of bowl, detaching custard from bowl. Place a round dessert plate over mold and invert to unmold. Pat gently and lift up mold. The custard will have a glaze of caramel over top and sides. Serve at once.

༆

EGG CUSTARD GELATO

Gelato di Crema

The Italian egg custard gelato is soft and voluptuous. Serve it alone or topped with some hot melted chocolate.

§◗ MAKES ABOUT 1 QUART

3 cups milk
8 large egg yolks
¾ cup sugar

Put milk in a medium saucepan and bring to just below a boil over medium heat; do not let it boil. Turn off heat.

Meanwhile put egg yolks and sugar in top part of a double boiler or heatproof bowl, and beat with a wire whisk or electric hand beater until pale yellow and thick. Gradually pour hot milk into beaten eggs in a thin stream, stirring constantly with whisk.

Place over a few inches of slowly simmering water (do not let water boil) and cook, stirring constantly with a spatula, until custard thickens and thickly coats back of a spoon, about 15 minutes.

Strain custard through a fine-mesh sieve into a clean bowl. Set bowl over a larger bowl of iced water and cool completely. Cover bowl and refrigerate until cold.

Freeze mixture in an ice-cream freezer according to manufacturer's instructions. Serve immediately or freeze until needed.

ALMOND COOKIES

Amaretti

Many of the trattorie in the Emilia farmland serve, at the end of a meal, fragrant, addictive homemade amaretti cookies. And many are the homes that keep these small cookies in their cupboard and serve them when an impromptu visitor shows up. When my husband and I spent a few days at Villa Gaidello, a lovely guest farm in the countryside of Castelfranco Emilia, a little plate of amaretti would materialize immediately each time we would sit down for a cappuccino or an espresso. This recipe comes from Villa Gaidello.

MAKES 25 TO 30

½ **pound blanched almonds (about 2 cups)**
2 **tablespoons plus ⅔ cup sugar**
2 **egg whites at room temperature**

Preheat oven to 350F (175C). Spread almonds on a baking sheet and bake until they are lightly toasted, about 2 minutes. Cool almonds and place in bowl of a food processor fitted with the metal blade. Add 2 tablespoons sugar and pulse machine on and off until almonds are very finely chopped but not pulverized. Set aside.

Reduce oven temperature to 325F (165C). Butter a large baking sheet and line it with parchment paper (the paper will be held in place by butter).

In a large bowl, mix chopped almonds and ½ cup of the sugar. Beat egg whites with remaining sugar until stiff peaks form, and fold them a little at a time into almonds.

Spoon up mixture with a tablespoon, filling it only halfway, and make small mounds on prepared baking sheet, leaving space between each mound. Place baking sheet on middle rack of oven and bake until amaretti are thoroughly dry, and they just begin to color, about 20 minutes. Cool completely before serving. They can be kept in a cookie jar for several days before serving.

ITALIAN RUM CAKE

Zuppa Inglese

This is one of Italy's most popular desserts.

§ MAKES 10 TO 12 SERVINGS

Fruit Salad

5 cups any prepared fruit in season

½ cup chopped candied fruit

2 tablespoons rum

3 tablespoons sugar

Hot Zabaglione, page 229, substituting ⅓
  cup rum for wine

1 cup whipping cream

12 ounces pound cake, cut into medium-
  thin slices

½ cup rum

Fresh strawberries and/or grated
  chocolate

Prepare Fruit Salad: Combine fresh fruit, candied fruit, rum and sugar in a medium bowl. Refrigerate until ready to use or up to several hours ahead.

Prepare Hot Zabaglione, using rum. Remove from heat and set pan or bowl containing mixture over a bowl full of ice water. Stir with a whisk until mixture is warm. Whip cream and fold it into warm mixture. Zabaglione can be prepared several hours ahead and set over a bowl of ice water until needed.

Arrange slices of pound cake in a large glass bowl. Sprinkle a little rum over each slice. Cover cake with a layer of Fruit Salad. Cover Fruit Salad with a generous amount of Zabaglione.

Continue layers until bowl is filled. Refrigerate overnight. Before serving, decorate with fresh strawberries and/or grated chocolate. Serve chilled.

MARIA ANGELA'S MERINGUE CAKE

Dolce di Maria Angela

This is a family favorite from my good friend Maria Angela di Massa.

MAKES 6 TO 8 SERVINGS

Meringues
4 egg whites, at room temperature
1 cup sugar
1 teaspoon vanilla extract
1 teaspoon white wine vinegar

Coffee Zabaglione
5 egg yolks

1 cup sugar
¼ cup espresso coffee or strong regular
　coffee, at room temperature

1 cup sweet butter, at room temperature
Candied violets

Prepare Meringues: Preheat oven to 275F (135C). Butter and flour 2 cookie sheets. In a large bowl, beat egg whites until stiff. Beat in 6 tablespoons of the sugar, 1 tablespoon at a time. Beat in vanilla and vinegar. Add remaining sugar, beating until egg whites are very stiff and shiny. Put egg white mixture into a pastry bag fitted with a medium star tube. Pipe mixture in small mounds onto prepared cookie sheets or shape into mounds using 2 spoons. Bake 1 hour. Turn off oven. Leave meringues in oven overnight with door closed. Store meringues in an airtight container. Meringues can be stored several weeks. Makes about 25 meringues.

Prepare Coffee Zabaglione: In a large bowl or the top part of a double boiler, beat egg yolks and sugar until pale and thick. Set bowl or top part of double boiler over simmering water; do not let water boil. Gradually add coffee, beating constantly. Continue beating until Zabaglione has doubled in volume and is soft and fluffy, 4 to 6 minutes. Remove from heat and set pan or bowl over a bowl full of ice water. Stir with a whisk until mixture is cool.

Cream butter in a large bowl until pale and fluffy. Gradually add cooled Zabaglione to butter, beating vigorously after each addition. Refrigerate 2 to 3 minutes to stiffen slightly.

On a large round platter, arrange about 8 meringues close together in a circle. Put Zabaglione mixture into a pastry bag fitted with a medium star tube. Pipe rosettes between meringues. Arrange another layer of meringues over the first, forming a smaller circle. Pipe rosettes of Zabaglione mixture between meringues. Repeat layers using remaining meringues and most of Zabaglione mixture to make a cone-shaped mound. Decorate cake with candied violets and remaining Zabaglione mixture. Refrigerate overnight. Let cake stand 30 minutes at room temperature before serving.

Seasonal Menus

One problem that confronts someone serving ethnic food for the first time is how to compose the menu. So many of my students ask me the same question: "I am planning a dinner party and I would like to make tortellini with cream sauce. What appetizer should I have and what dessert should I serve?"

The success of a meal depends not only on how well the food is prepared but also on how the menu is put together. In a way it is like listening to a beautiful piece of music. Each note can be played perfectly but the overall beauty of the sound depends on the way the notes are put together. To prepare a beautiful meal you must start by planning a beautiful menu: A menu in which each dish complements the other. One that takes advantage of seasonal ingredients and suits the mood of the time of year.

An Italian meal moves through its many courses in a leisurely and orderly sequence. Wine is always present. The right wine not only complements the meal, but enhances appreciation of it. On a hot summer day we eat differently than in winter. It would be ridiculous to spend time over a hot stove, stirring a bubbling polenta when the temperature outside reaches the sizzling point. On the other hand, cook a polenta on a cold winter day and you bring a warm glow to your family or guests. With this concept in mind, I have put together menus for this chapter. They are divided into spring and summer, and fall and winter. These menus are intended only as guidelines because there are countless possible menu combinations using the recipes in this book.

By changing a pasta dish, by substituting meat for fish, by eliminating a course, you can create your own menus. Each combination can fit a particular occasion or season. For example, a pot of bean soup followed by broiled chicken or Chicken Hunter Style, page 122, can become a simple yet excellent meal. Serve it for an informal gathering of friends. Why not cook several frittatas, make a tomato and basil salad and fill a cheese board with assorted Italian cheeses? Then eat this delightful meal informally outdoors on your patio, by a river or at a beach. Select a stuffed pasta dish and, working around it, build an elegant meal—a meal that will linger in the minds of your guests. And let's not forget the everyday meals for our families. The same care should be taken in preparing the simplest of meals. After all, good food should not be kept in the closet and served only on special occasions. Good food belongs on the everyday table. We must all eat, so why not make the best of it?

Most Italian meals end with an unbeatable combination—cheese and fruit. Creamy Gorgonzola cheese and sweet, ripe pears is a marriage made in heaven. Fresh fruit, when ripe and sweet, can stand on its own as dessert. Of course there are many occasions when a beautiful dessert should end a meal. In formal entertaining, a spectacular dessert is not only advised, but recommended. If you plan a menu with a beautiful first course and end with an impressive dessert, you can be sure your dinner party will be a success.

To end an Italian meal without espresso coffee would be an absurdity. In Italy, espresso is a national institution. I remember when my husband first arrived in Bologna to attend medical school, he barely managed one or two cups of this strong coffee a day. By the time he graduated, he was drinking eight to ten cups a day. Today, after 30 years in this country I still start my day with several cups of espresso and end it in the same way. Many of my friends believe espresso is the source of my considerable energy.

The menus start with one really lavish holiday menu from Emilia-Romagna.

It just occurred to me that this is the last chapter of this book. After working on it for more than a year, I know I will miss the daily routine of preparing recipes in my kitchen and then sitting down to write them up. I hope I have achieved what I had in mind. I set out to share with you not only some of the food of northern Italy, but also to give you a little understanding of a very old, warm and beautiful country.

HOLIDAY MENU FROM EMILIA-ROMAGNA

Prosciutto with melon

Green Tagliatelle with Tomato Sauce, page 50

Stuffed Veal Roast, page 155

Stuffed Artichokes, page 185

Baked Tomatoes, page 180

Buttered carrots

Oranges in liqueur

Sweet Fried Cream, page 230

Mature Barbaresco or Cabernet Sauvignon

FALL AND WINTER MENUS

Pan-Roasted Chicken, page 115

Peas with Prosciutto, page 184

Fresh fruit

Jam Tart, page 218

Vapolicella or Gamay Beaujolais

. . .

Hot Anchovy Dip, page 17

Basic Polenta, page 86, with Rabbit with Wine and Vegetables, page 117

Mixed Salad, page 196

Pears Poached in Red Wine, page 218

Barbera or Cabernet Sauvignon

SPRING AND SUMMER MENUS

Trenette with Pesto Sauce, page 74

Cold Veal in Tuna Sauce, page 154

Mixed Salad, page 196

Cold Zabaglione, page 229, with fresh strawberries

Trebbiano or Fumé Blanc

. . .

Rice and Pea Soup, page 31

Calf's Liver in Onion Sauce, page 145

Asparagus Salad, page 195

Sweet Fried Cream, page 230, with fresh fruit

Merlot, Light Mendocino or Zinfandel

. . .

Strichetti with Garlic and Tomato Sauce, page 58

Veal Chops Milan Style, page 148

Mushrooms with Marsala Wine and Cream, page 178

Mixed Salad, page 196

Gattinara or Pinot Noir

. . .

Risotto with Asparagus Tips, page 100

Tomato Salad, page 192

Trout in Foil, page 104

Fried Fruit, page 226

Gavi dei Gavi or Chardonnay

. . .

Prosciutto with figs

Spaghetti with Spring Vegetables, page 63

Roast Rack of Lamb, page 130

Zucchini with Vinegar, page 177

Strawberry Mousse, page 220

Tignanello or Cabernet Sauvignon

METRIC CONVERSION CHARTS

COMPARISON TO METRIC MEASURE

When you know	Symbol	Multiply By	To Find	Symbol
teaspoons	tsp.	5.0	milliliters	ml
tablespoons	tbsp.	15.0	milliliters	ml
fluid ounces	fl.oz.	30.0	milliliters	ml
cups	c	0.24	liters	l
pints	pt.	0.47	liters	l
quarts	qt.	0.95	liters	l
ounces	oz.	28.0	grams	g
pounds	lb.	0.45	kilograms	kg
Fahrenheit	F	5/9 (after subtracting 32)	Celsius	C

FAHRENHEIT TO CELSIUS

F	C
200-205	95
220-225	105
245-250	120
275	135
300-305	150
325-330	165
345-350	175
370-375	190
400-405	205
425-430	220
445-450	230
470-475	245
500	260

LIQUID MEASURE TO MILLILITERS

1/4 teaspoon	=	1.25	milliliters
1/2 teaspoon	=	2.5	milliliters
3/4 teaspoon	=	3.75	milliliters
1 teaspoon	=	5.0	milliliters
1-1/4 teaspoons	=	6.25	milliliters
1-1/2 teaspoons	=	7.5	milliliters
1-3/4 teaspoons	=	8.75	milliliters
2 teaspoons	=	10.0	milliliters
1 tablespoon	=	15.0	milliliters
2 tablespoons	=	30.0	milliliters

LIQUID MEASURE TO LITERS

1/4 cup	=	0.06	liters
1/2 cup	=	0.12	liters
3/4 cup	=	0.18	liters
1 cup	=	0.24	liters
1-1/4 cups	=	0.3	liters
1-1/2 cups	=	0.36	liters
2 cups	=	0.48	liters
2-1/2 cups	=	0.6	liters
3 cups	=	0.72	liters
3-1/2 cups	=	0.84	liters
4 cups	=	0.96	liters
4-1/2 cups	=	1.08	liters
5 cups	=	1.2	liters
5-1/2 cups	=	1.32	liters

English Index

245

Italian Index

About the Author

Biba Caggiano is the award-winning author of seven cookbooks, all of which are still in print. Her cookbooks have sold over 600,000 copies. She is the host of the syndicated cooking show *Biba's Italian Kitchen* on The Learning Channel. The show is seen in several countries, including Canada and Australia.

She has been the chef/owner of Biba restaurant in Sacramento, California, since 1986. The restaurant has been featured in *Gourmet, Bon Appétit* and *Travel & Leisure*. In 1998, the governor of California and the California Travel Industry selected Biba as the Northern California Chef of the Year.

Originally from the Emilia-Romagna region of Italy, she now lives in California.